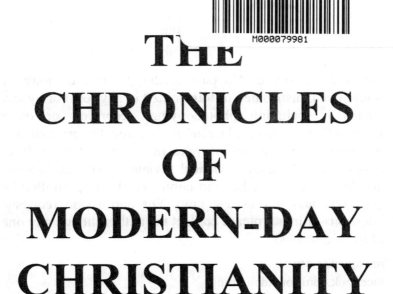

# THE CHRONICLES OF MODERN-DAY CHRISTIANITY

## THE EVANGELIZATION OF THE NATIONS IN THIS GENERATION

### Ronald C. Harding, Jr.

The Chronicles Of Modern-Day Christianity
Ron Harding
ISBN: 9781792042409

First Print – 2nd Edition

# TABLE OF CONTENTS

# FORWARD

One of the most shocking facts about Christianity is that the very "way" to become a Christian was lost for the greater part of 1,500 years. From the Edict of Milan in 313AD when Emperor Constantine ushered in what became the Catholic Church to the 16th century when the "Radical Reformers" in Europe influenced the "Anabaptists," we do not know of any movement that made disciples and baptized them for the forgiveness of their sins. Even the brutally persecuted Anabaptists, some of whom briefly seem to have made disciples and baptized them for the remission of sins, devolved into obscurity and legalism, eventually moving away from this salvation doctrine thus becoming the Amish, Mennonites and Hutterites.

Therefore, from the fourth century to the present the history of "Christianity" is mostly devoid of one thing, Christians! Catholics were born Catholics and later Protestants were born Protestants. Neither traditions contained Peter's true call to simply, *"Repent and be baptized, every one of you, in the name of Jesus Christ for the forgiveness of your sins."* (Acts 2:38) For generations the simple yet powerful truths of how to become a Christian had been carefully hidden and confused by Satan. Even though God called out in each generation (Acts 17:27), no man answered the call to take the Gospel to the ends of the earth as the Apostles had done. (Acts 1:8)

Yet by the grace of God, in America in the early 1800's the Spirit of the Lord moved in the hearts of men to reignite the fire of true discipleship. Barton Stone was the leader of the "Cane Ridge Revival" in Lexington, Kentucky where from August 6-12, 1801 over 20,000 people came to hear the preaching of many ministers and receive communion. It was an incredible moment; some called it the American Pentecost! In an effort to build a powerful church and make many Christians in a world he considered polluted by false doctrine and sectarianism in 1803, Stone and others formed the Springfield Presbytery. However, in Stone's effort to build a powerful church, he realized that in fact all he was doing was building another denomination. Therefore in 1804, he and several others published the *Last Will And Testament Of The Springfield Presbytery*. This document announced their withdrawal from denominationalism and the accompanying creeds and traditions that supported it. They wished to "be dissolved and sink into union with the Body of Christ at large; for there is but one body, and one Spirit, even as we are called in one hope of our calling." Barton Stone set out on a mission to uncover the original beliefs and practices of the First Century Church. Through these events, Barton Stone became the leader of a movement and one of the earliest voices of non-denominationalism.

Another Minister, Thomas Campbell, an Irish immigrant to America penned the document known as the *Declaration And Address* in 1809. It was a call to unity among Christians and a return to the model and teachings of the "First Century" / "New Testament" Church. Thomas's son Alexander Campbell was deeply impacted by his father's teachings and became a leader in what then became the embryonic "Restoration Movement." He yearned for a return to the "ancient order" of the church and Christianity. He once wrote, "I labor to see sectarianism abolished, and all Christians of every name united upon the one foundation on which the Apostolic Church was founded."

In their effort to return to the genuine teachings of the Bible and reject the creeds and traditions that had so poisoned the denominational world, this father and son duel stumbled over a hidden teaching for centuries – "repentance and baptism for the remission of sins!" (Acts 2:38) Alexander Campbell wrote, "Baptism for the remission of sins is the only baptism of which the New Testament knows anything." The Campbells were baptized by immersion on June 12, 1812 by the Baptist pastor Matthias Luce at Buffalo Creek, West Virginia. When asked if baptism was a "work" Alexander replied, "We do not place baptism among good

8

works. In baptism we are passive in everything but giving our consent." God had moved in an incredible way in His abundant grace to re-initiate true Christianity.

In 1821 the Campbells met with another powerful reformer, preacher and evangelist, Walter Scott. Scott had been baptized by immersion in 1819 and believed that baptism was for the forgiveness of sins. Walter Scott was a very dynamic preacher and joined them in spreading the message. In 1824, the Campbells and Barton Stone met and found that they agreed Biblically on so much that by 1832 their movements had merged into one. Their voices joined the growing chorus of preachers and Bible students who yearned to return to true Christianity, which they now started to call "Discipleship."

The Restoration Movement grew and thrived for over 60 years, and there is much to say about its great colleges, congregations and publications. However, because of Darwinism and the destructive "higher criticism" of the Bible coming from German theologians, the "liberal" Disciples of Christ denomination began to evolve into a separate fellowship in the 1860's. Then formally in 1906, Satan had sewn so many seeds of dissent and discord that the Restoration Movement split again into the (Conservative) Christian Churches and (Mainline) Churches of Christ over the issue of instrumental music in the church; the Christian Churches believed that instruments in the worship service were permissible, but the Churches of Christ believed it to be sin. These ministries had varying degrees of success, and yet, because both practiced the church governess of local autonomy, the powerful message of salvation was largely blocked from wide-scale international expansion. Also, in the Restoration Movement never was every "Christian" given the training or the tools to make a Christian. The conversion process was for the most part handled by the full-time, male ministry staff.

Much like the legend of Excalibur, the *"sword of the Word"* (Ephesians 6:17) had become encased in stone. Baptisms became very few and people lost their understanding, faith and gratitude for the ability they had to make disciples. The stone that locked Excalibur was, in this case, the cold and hard hearts of men.

Many years would pass, but God will never cease to reach-out to mankind. At 1:30am on April 11, 1972, Kip McKean was baptized for the forgiveness of sins in the "experimental" campus ministry of the 14th Street Church of Christ – one year later renamed the Crossroads Church of Christ. After being trained at the Crossroads Church, the Harding Graduate School of Religion, and by God's hand in day-to-day ministry, Kip understood the power of the gift he had been given – the ability to baptize people into Christ and make totally committed disciples. He answered God's call and understood the magnitude of this "discovery." Like the young King Arthur, he "pulled the sword from the stone" and began to dream of an evangelized world.

God worked in many ways to season and prepare Kip for the work that He had prepared for him, but finally in 1979, he took the helm of the Lexington Church of Christ in Massachusetts. Kip's first direction to the church was that "every member" – adults, singles, campus and teens – were to be "totally committed." In 1980, to help his congregation to grow spiritually and numerically, Kip developed a Bible Study Series called *First Principles*. For the first time in about 2,000 years every disciple could make a disciple... Up until that time the Restoration Movement had been like Israel in 1 Samuel 13:19, *"Not a blacksmith could be found in the whole land of Israel, because the Philistines had said, 'Otherwise the Hebrews will make swords or spears!'"* Now every disciple had the ability and encouragement to "swing the sword" and impact their classmates and neighbors!

This is an excerpt from Ron Harding's incredible book *The Chronicles of Modern-Day Christianity:*

*During the ten years that the McKeans served the Boston Church of Christ, the Spirit produced exponential growth! The original Lexington Church of Christ had witnessed only two baptisms in the previous three years before June 1, 1979. Through the restoration of the radical call and practice that every member of the congregation is "totally committed," the Boston Church of Christ had 103 baptisms the first year! The most dynamic and well-established Mainline Church of Christ for decades had only baptized 200 to 300 each year. In fact, during the 80's, every year a list of Mainline Churches of Christ baptizing 100 or more was published which usually had only 15 Mainline Churches listed. With God's Spirit working through the McKeans, the Boston Church of Christ saw exactly 200 baptisms their second year; 256 their third; 368 in the fourth; 457 in the fifth; 679 in the sixth; 735 in the seventh; 947 in the eighth; 1424 in the ninth; and in the Boston Church's tenth year 1621 were baptized into Christ. By this time also, the Sunday attendance in Boston was approaching 4,000 as the church met in the famed Boston Garden – "home" of the Boston Celtics professional basketball team. Not only was this the largest single congregation in the history of New England, but it also became the largest "Church of Christ" in the entire world!*

From Boston, the Holy Spirit sent out "discipling churches" that spread over the world reaching 171 of the world's 196 nations. Through Kip, the Holy Spirit would restore New Testament disciple-making in the 20th century not only in Boston, but worldwide! However, Satan attacked and destroyed that movement. Now in the early years of the 21st century, the spirit revived Kip and thus the disciple-making movement – now called the SoldOut Movement or the International Christian Churches! There is much history to read and I wholeheartedly recommend Ron's book. As Luke

11

in the Book of Acts recorded the Movement of God in the first century, so Ron has recorded the Movement of God in the 20th and 21st centuries! And to God be all the glory!

Dr. Timothy C. Kernan

# OVERVIEW

*"Then Jesus turned to His disciples and said privately, 'Blessed are the eyes that see what you see. For I tell you that many prophets and kings wanted to see what you see but did not see it, and to hear what you hear but did not hear it.'"* **Luke 10:23-24**

The primary purposes of this exciting narration are to honor God with the truth and to encourage those who have never had the dream – or perhaps have lost it – to share in Jesus' dream of the "evangelization of all nations in this generation." (1 Timothy 2:3-4) Since we live in an age in which the proliferation of information is often distorted, I have sought to carefully investigate and document with first-hand accounts – including my own – the incredible story of the spread of true Christianity from the 1970's to this very day. This rich history is intertwined with the life of my *"partner in the Gospel"* Kip McKean – known as a preacher, missionary, reformer, theologian and humanitarian.

Kip McKean visited Smokey Mountain in
Metro Manila for the first time in 1989!

Just as the Bible used the biographies of Abraham, Moses, David, Jesus and Paul as timelines, so I have used Kip's many experiences as a timeline – his faith, his faults and his rekindled fire – to allow me to render a detailed and *"orderly [historical] account."* (Luke 1:1-4; Acts 1:1)

Dr. Thomas Wayne McKean II (May 31, 1954 – present) was named after his ancestor Thomas McKean, who was a signer of the Declaration of Independence. (His mother nicknamed him "Kip" on the day he was born.) In 2003, Kip became the Evangelist for the Portland International Church of Christ. In October 2006, after a valiant three-year effort to bring reform to the crumbling International Churches of Christ (ICOC), the Holy Spirit used Kip, soon joined by other valiant disciples on every continent, to initiate the new Portland / SoldOut Discipling Movement!

In May 2007, Kip and Elena McKean – alongside 40 other disciples from Portland – planted the City of Angels International Christian Church, which now has 1,300 at their Sunday Services! Kip serves as the "World Missions Evangelist" for the International Christian Churches – now the fastest spreading Christian movement in the world! Another milestone was achieved in 2012, as decades of dreams and prayers were fulfilled with the founding of the International College of Christian Ministries (ICCM) in Los Angeles. Amazingly, accredited Bachelor's, Master's and Doctorate Degrees are granted according to the SoldOut Movement's convictions. Kip serves as the Chancellor of ICCM-Global overseeing ICCM-Los Angeles and extension campuses in Boston, Columbus, Lagos, Manila, Miami, New York City, Portland, São Paulo, Toronto and Washington DC.

Of note in 1979, Kip and Elena were invited to lead the Lexington Church of Christ (later renamed the Boston Church of Christ). From these "30 would-be-disciples," the Spirit ignited a movement of churches known as the Boston Movement and in 1994 renamed the International Churches of Christ (ICOC). Kip's tenacious embrace of Jesus' radical dream "to evangelize the nations in a generation," his bold

14

theological reforms, his personal warmth coupled with his charismatic and uncompromising Bible preaching, allowed the Spirit to take the Gospel from one small dying church in Boston in 1979 to become by 2001 – the year of his sabbatical – almost 400 churches in 171 of the 196 nations of the world! Then as this noble effort was being tragically decimated in 2001, 2002 and 2003, God sent Kip on a rocky path of suffering and redemption. For nearly two years, he wandered in a lonely, spiritual wilderness, which greatly humbled him. Yet, those dark days ultimately strengthened Kip's resolve to fulfill "the dream." Therefore in 2018, it is so amazing that in just 11 years, God's new SoldOut Movement has almost 100 congregations in 38 nations... and counting! From a historical perspective, no other preacher in the past century has been directly responsible for the planting of so many congregations around the world!

Concerning "the evangelization of the nations in this generation," some in the ICOC have asked, "What is going to be different this 'second time' around?" This presupposes the question, "Can it be different this second time?" The answer in the Scriptures is a resounding yes! The first time the Israelites approached the Promised Land, their lack of faith led them to the dreadful desires to choose a different leader than the one God had chosen and to return to their lives of slavery in Egypt. This unbelief ultimately resulted in their death in the desert. The second time the Spirit led the Israelites to the border of the Promised Land, the Hebrew people – having learned to rely on God in their wanderings in the desert – now succeeded to make God's dream and promise a reality. This same learning from the past prayerfully will continue to be true for God's new SoldOut Movement. As Kip preached at the 2010 Jubilee on the theme of The Promised Land On The Second Try, "Second is best because God rewards the quest"*

*Red text denotes most of the critical issues and events surrounding the Chronicles of Modern-Day Christianity.

# EARLY LIFE AND FAMILY

Kip McKean was born in Indianapolis, Indiana on May 31, 1954. Like many young men of the 1960's, he was inspired by those who refused to compromise and were willing to sacrifice everything for a worthy cause. This temperament is also deep in the McKean family heritage, as they are called higher by the courage of one of their ancestors, Thomas McKean. As with all of the "Signers of the Declaration of Independence," death threats were common. Interestingly, Thomas McKean not only was a "Signer" for Delaware, but also was "the President" of the Congress of Confederation – the highest office in the new United States of America – when news arrived from General Washington that the British had surrendered!

Kip's father, serving as an admiral in the U.S. Navy, became a strong influence, an early role model for leadership and excellence, and Kip's first hero. His mother, a very talented artist, nurtured in him an uncommon warmth, as well as a character of resilience.

Both of Kip's parents – Tom and Kim McKean –
celebrated their 80th Birthdays in 2008!

Between the ages of seven and 16, every summer Kip alongside his beloved younger brother Randy and dear

17

younger sister Dana spent one month with each set of grandparents – "Grampy and Grammy" and "Grandpa and Grandma." Those days with his grandparents in Michigan and Indiana respectively heightened his sense of adventure and deepened his love and appreciation of family.

During his high school years – in Virginia Beach, Virginia; Winter Park, Florida; and Libertyville, Illinois – Kip played varsity football, was selected to be a member of the National Honor Society, and also obtained the rank of Eagle in the Boy Scouts. During these formative years, Kip's heroes became John F. Kennedy and Dr. Martin Luther King Jr. However, in time, Kip's greatest hero became Jesus.

# MARRIAGE AND CHILDREN

Kip married Elena Garcia-Bengochea on December 11, 1976. Elena was born in Havana, Cuba on September 2, 1955 and fled with her family to the United States in a boat in 1959. Growing up in Gainesville, Florida, Elena attended P. K. Yonge High School. She distinguished herself as a straight-A student, Student Body Treasurer, Captain of the Tennis Team, Captain of the Varsity Cheerleaders, and Homecoming Queen.

At 17, Elena was baptized into Christ the summer before her freshman year at the University of Florida on August 8, 1973. Kip and Elena met at the Crossroads Church of Christ and were married on December 11, 1976.

Kip and Elena were married on
December 11, 1976!

19

The McKeans' wedding began a
lifetime full of adventure!

In 1981, they welcomed their first child – Olivia. Then in
1982 and 1984 respectively, Sean and Eric were born. Very
inspirationally, since all three of the McKean children were
born on the fifth floor of the small Mount Auburn Hospital
– less than a mile from Harvard University, Kip began to
pray daily for all three to attend Harvard University. The
strong characters of the McKeans' children, as well as their
godly upbringing, are illustrated by the fact that Olivia and
Sean graduated from Harvard and Eric, though accepted at
Harvard, chose to attend and then graduated from Stanford
University, where he served as Captain of the renowned
Stanford Tennis Team. Kip and Elena viewed these events
as God having honored Kip's prayer, since all three children
were "accepted" to Harvard! (Their educations were funded
through the combination of the McKeans' small savings,

Kip's parents, close friends of the McKeans, and scholarships – both academic and athletic, as well as financial aid.)

Sean, Olivia and Eric in 1990 in Los Angeles!

Eric, Olivia and Sean in 2008!

Through the years, through all their individual trials, the McKeans remain an extremely happy and tight-knit family. All three children have married and have very successful careers. Kip and Elena are now tremendously excited to be grandparents!

"Abuelo Kip" and one of his three beloved
granddaughters – Scarlett!

# HIGH SCHOOL AND COLLEGE YEARS

Prior to high school, Kip was not religious. However, at the end of Kip's sophomore year in high school, he became very involved in a dynamic fundamental Christian congregation in Maitland, Florida – the Asbury United Methodist Church. Here he came to a deep personal faith in Christ and in the divine inspiration of the Bible.

The Asbury United Methodist Church of Maitland,
Florida where Kip was first influenced
to study the Bible!

In March of his freshman year at the University of Florida, he was invited to a college devotional sponsored by the 14th Street Church of Christ. (A year later, this congregation adopted the name of the Crossroads Church of Christ.) This congregation in Gainesville had begun a pilot program for campus ministry for the Mainline Churches of Christ just five years earlier in 1967. Some of the more progressive Mainline Churches of Christ desired to impact the secular college campuses of America and initially modeled their efforts after Campus Crusade. They called this new program

23

– led by Chuck Lucas – Campus Advance. Here Kip was taught to give up everything for Christ and be baptized for the remission of sins to become a Christian. As a 17-year old freshman, Kip made this commitment and was baptized at 1:30AM on April 11, 1972.

For summer vacation in 1972, Kip returned home to Chicago. He became very sick; boils covered the entire upper part of his body. Bandages were wrapped around his body for the next three months. He believes that at that time God was testing and humbling him, particularly through the scarring on his face. Of note, the members of the Mainline Church of Christ that he attended in the Chicago area never came to visit him while he was sick. This incident in his life sensitized him to meeting people's needs, particularly visiting the sick. Later that summer, even though the doctors strongly advised Kip otherwise because of his weakened health, he returned to Gainesville so that he could once again participate in a strong fellowship of college Christians.

During his sophomore year in college, though involved in the High Honors Chemistry Pre-med Program at the University of Florida, Kip began to dream about becoming a campus minister. God reinforced this dream when his brother Randy was diagnosed with cancer (Hodgkin's Lymphoma) in the spring of 1973. Kip baptized his brother six months later. (His sister Dana was baptized 15 years later.) Kip's Christianity also led to conflict where he lived in the Sigma Chi Fraternity House. That same year, his stand for purity almost led to his dismissal from the fraternity. However, many of his fellow fraternity brothers rallied around him electing him "Tribune." Also, during his three years of living in the fraternity house, he hosted a weekly Bible Study in his room, through which eight of his fraternity brothers and several others were baptized into Christ. These events solidified Kip's sense that God was calling him into the full-time ministry, thus sacrificing the much more lucrative lifestyle of a doctor.

24

In 1973, Kip heard the voice of God and
decided to go into the ministry!

While attending the Crossroads Church of Christ, the vision
of dynamic campus ministries throughout America was put
on Kip's heart. He was inspired by the powerful preaching
of Chuck Lucas and his associate Sam Laing. Kip was also
stirred by their innovations derived from Biblical principles:
"prayer partners" – based on the "one another" Scriptures;
"counting the cost" with each individual before baptism
from Luke 14:25-33; and evangelistic small group Bible
studies called "Soul Talks." At this point, the seeds of
discipling were placed in his life as he personally saw how

one man could affect another's daily lifestyle and eternal destiny for God. During these early years of the "Crossroads Movement" – also known as the "Total Commitment Movement" – the Crossroads Church and the young ministers they sent out became more and more controversial within the Mainline Churches of Christ, because of these innovations and the call to be "totally committed." In some cases, these "Crossroads Campus Ministry Churches" were "disfellowshipped" or "marked" by the "other" Mainline Churches of Christ.

# GOD'S PREPARATION AND EDUCATION

In June 1975, Kip graduated from the University of Florida with High Honors as well as being selected to the most well-known of all scholastic honorary fraternities – Phi Beta Kappa. In September 1975, the Spirit guided Kip to Philadelphia where he was hired as the Campus Minister for Northeastern Christian College (NCC) – a Mainline Church of Christ school. Here he saw first-hand how uncommitted many of the so-called "Christian students" were; drugs, drunkenness, prejudice, impurity and immorality were prevalent. He came to a deep conviction that being religious is not the same as being a righteous and true follower of Jesus.

Kip first served in the full-time ministry as the Campus Minister for Northeastern Christian College in September 1975!

27

While Kip was serving as the Campus Minister at NCC, the King of Prussia Church of Christ gave him a scholarship to attend Eastern Baptist Theological Seminary. There he was challenged by one of his professors, the Dean of Academics, that the Bible is not the "only" inspired Word of God. Shocked, yet sure in his faith, Kip zealously responded to the Dean's challenge, "If there are any other holy writings beside the Bible, then Christianity is reduced to simply another philosophy like Confucianism, Islam, Buddhism or Hinduism. To me, Christ and His Word are the only way, the only truth and the only life." This core conviction has guided Kip during his 43 years of full-time ministry. As with Jesus, the Apostles and all of God's prophets, Kip has been persecuted with countless death threats, as well as publicly chastised in TV shows, on the internet, and in magazines and newspapers for his "narrow view" of the Bible and salvation. (Matthew 7:13-14, Acts 4:12) Yet, he has never wavered in his convictions about Jesus as the Christ and the inspiration of the Old and New Testament Scriptures.

In the fall of 1976, Kip began to serve the Lord at the Heritage Chapel Church of Christ in Charleston, Illinois. He was asked to initiate a campus ministry at Eastern Illinois University – a small college of 9,300 students. During his three years there – starting with just seven college students – God blessed his ministry with 300 campus baptisms!

Interestingly, Illinois was considered a "mission field" of the Mainline Churches of Christ, as the Mainline Churches were and still are largely concentrated in America's Southern States – the "Bible Belt." Kip was supported "as a missionary" by the Memorial Church of Christ in Houston, Texas. After eight months, some of the elders of the Memorial Church visited the Heritage Chapel Church. Instead of rejoicing at the large number of campus converts, they were "appalled" by the clapping during the singing of devotional songs, women praying in mixed groups, and the overall fervor of the worship service. Accused of "Pentecostalism," "brain-washing," and "cult-like

28

practices," Kip was fired by the Memorial Church two weeks later. Yet inside of the Heritage Chapel Church, the members were very appreciative and loyal.

During their second year in Illinois, Kip and
Elena visited Elena's extended family –
the Garcia-Bengochea Familia!

God blessed the church's Biblical convictions from Kip's preaching as financial support was quickly found from the Union Avenue Church of Christ in Memphis, Tennessee. In return for Kip serving in the Union Avenue Church in the summers, the Union Avenue Church generously gave Kip not only yearly financial support, but also a full scholarship to Harding Graduate School of Religion, the most high-profile of all the "Mainline Church of Christ seminaries."

# REVOLUTIONARY THE*O*LOGY

Continuing his quest of a Masters in Theology which he began at Eastern Baptist Theological Seminary, Kip attended Harding Graduate School for two summers. He concluded that though helpful in scholastic pursuits, a formal seminary – where future ministers' days were consumed with their academics and so were "removed" from being immersed in the lives of people – was not the way to train evangelists. Rather, it is one minster walking with another like Jesus with His Twelve or Paul training Timothy and Titus. Yet, Kip especially appreciated his courses in church history and in the Old Testament, and so began to dream of a way to have day-to-day training in ministry combined with Bible courses. (Later of great value in Kip's in-depth, scholarly Bible studies was taking one year of Greek at the University of Florida, where he received an "A" for all three quarters.)

Well documented in the 1970's was that an "average" Mainline Church of Christ congregation had 150 members and only eight baptisms per year. Six of these baptisms were children of the members and the others were baptized from the world. A majority of the members' children left the church, and over 90% of the other baptisms fell away.

Later in 1986, Flavil Yeakley reported in his book *Why Churches Grow* that Mac Lynn's first accurate survey of the Mainline Churches of Christ revealed only 965,439 actual members as opposed to the 2.5 million that had been claimed. He discovered that instead of an estimated 15,000 congregations, there were actually only 10,165 Mainline Churches of Christ in America. Lynn recorded, "The Churches of Christ have only 24 churches with a membership of 1,000 or more, only four with a membership of 2,000 or more, and only one with a membership of more than 3,000." The largest Mainline Church of Christ outside the borders of the United States was only 500 in attendance. Yeakley also wrote, "In 1980, the Church of Christ in the United States started decreasing in total membership [through fall aways and an escalating death rate in an aging membership]. It is clear that if the 1965-1980 trend were to continue unchanged, the Church of Christ would cease to exist in this nation in just a few years."

In *The Code Blue Church of Christ Article* of November 14, 2018, Steve Gardner shared from *21st Century Christian* – a publication that tracks Church of Christ demographics – the astounding rate of the loss of membership and congregations: "The Churches of Christ have shrunk by an average of 930 adherents a month, every single month [from the year 2000 to 2017]; and about five Church of Christ congregations dissolved every month, on average, during that time frame." Again, using the *21st Century Christian* stats, Gardner indicated that there has been a greatly accelerated rate from 2014 to 2017. Sadly, in the Churches of Christ, "…over 2,000 people [are] departing and over nine congregations dissolving each and every month, on average, for the last three years."

It was into this stalled storm of uncommitment in the Churches of Christ, that Kip became the Campus Minister for the 100-member Heritage Chapel Church of Christ in September 1976. In fact, the senior minister of the Heritage Chapel Church was only able to baptize a few adults, as the adult membership remained lukewarm. So, during Kip's time in Charleston, he came to a conviction that no matter how dynamic a campus ministry is, unless a whole church is "totally committed" the campus ministry's impact will be limited. From Kip's experiences and travels, he observed that many Mainline Churches of Christ with campus ministers from Crossroads had split, because of the committed college ministry exposing the uncommitment of the adult ministry. Shockingly, some preachers felt so threatened by these "successful" young campus ministers that they even preached from the pulpit against aspects of the campus ministry. In time, several of these young campus ministers sent out from the Crossroad Church became discouraged, and in turn, quit the ministry. In time, Kip

31

would preach, *"No one pours new wine into old wineskins. If he does, the new wine will burst the skins, the wine will run out and the wineskins will be ruined. No, new wine must be poured into new wineskins."* (Luke 5:37-38) Thus, Kip concluded through prayer and Bible study that the best way to build churches where every member is "totally committed" is to start new churches – for *"new wine [zealous young ministers] must be poured into new wineskins [new churches]."*

In Kip's years at Charleston and Memphis, he devoted himself to studying the Old Testament. This became a major turning point in Kip's revolutionary theology. First of all, he came to a deep conviction that unlike the Mainline Church of Christ whose plea was to be a "New Testament Church," a better understanding of God's eternal plan and His Word would create a "Bible Church." Kip fully realized that the Law – *"the written code, with its regulations"* from the Old Testament, was *"nailed to the cross"* thus nullifying it. (Colossians 2:14-15) However, Kip taught from 2 Timothy 3:16, *"All Scripture is God-breathed and is useful for teaching, rebuking, correcting and training in righteousness."* The word *"Scripture"* in the context of this passage refers only to the Old Testament. Therefore, the clear intent by Paul was to call Timothy – and all disciples – to use the Old Testament *"Scriptures"* in their preaching, in their discipling, and in their lives.

Secondly, Kip came to differ with the Mainline Church of Christ "doctrine" on Bible interpretation. In the early 1800's, Thomas Campbell – one of the founders of the Restoration Movement, which is the heritage of the Mainline Church of Christ – gave the Mainline Church of Christ the following creed: "Speak where the Bible speaks, and be silent where the Bible is silent." This creed dictated that one must have specific authorization by command, example or necessary inference only from the New Testament in order to implement a teaching or practice. However, Kip – believing that both the New Testament and Old Testament should be the foundation of the church – coined a phrase in sharp contrast to the Mainline's approach to interpretation. Kip taught Christians should be: "Silent where the Bible speaks, and speak where the Bible is silent." In other words, a Christian should simply obey where the Bible speaks, and may speak (have opinions) where the Bible is silent. This particular piece of Kip's revolutionary theology freed Christians to implement any practice or apply any name that is not prohibited in the Bible.

These two revolutionary concepts about the Scriptures were the fundamental reasons that many Mainline Churches of Christ opposed Kip. Ironically, though he is regarded by most as the "Founder of the International Churches of Christ," when in the early 2000's after the ICOC had returned to a more Mainline Church of Christ theological stance, because Kip continued to hold these same convictions, these revolutionary views of Scripture were the underlying causes for most of the leaders of the ICOC to vehemently oppose Kip and God's new SoldOut Discipling Movement.

# THE BOSTON MOVEMENT BEGINS

In November 1978, in what would become the McKeans' last six months in Charleston, the Elders of the Lexington Church of Christ in Massachusetts contacted Kip to be their pulpit minister, as well as their campus minister. At that time, this Mainline Church of Christ was desperate for a new direction as they were considering closing their doors, because their number had shrunk to about 60 members. When the McKeans interviewed for the position, Kip expressed to the elders in the Lexington congregation that in order for Elena and him to come, the elders would need to support him in calling "every member" – adults, singles, campus and teens – to be "totally committed." After over six long months of deliberation and "talks," the elders believed that God had not given them any other alternative, so they unanimously invited the young 25-year-old preacher to lead them!

Driving all night from Charleston to Boston, the McKeans arrived in the morning of Friday, June 1, 1979. So, in this small dying congregation, history was made that fateful evening, as "30 would-be disciples" gathered with enormous expectations in the living-room of members Bob and Pat Gempel to hear Kip's first lesson! At this point, the Lexington Church was simply viewed as another congregation of the "Crossroads" or "Total Commitment Movement." The profound difference between the Lexington Church and the other "Crossroads Ministries" would soon become apparent as Kip's revolutionary call from the Bible was for every member of the church to be "totally committed," not just the campus students.

In 1980, to help his congregation to grow spiritually and numerically, Kip developed a Bible Study Series called *First Principles*. (Hebrews 5:12; 6:1-3 WEV) Every member of the church was called to memorize these studies and then use the *First Principles Studies* to teach non-Christians the original standards that God had for individuals to become disciples of Christ. Perhaps the most radical and impacting study of the series was called *Discipleship*. In this study, Kip taught from Acts 11:26, SAVED = CHRISTIAN = DISCIPLE. Simply meaning that you cannot be saved and one is not a true Christian without being a baptized disciple. (John 4:1-2; Acts 2:38-42) Kip developed the *Discipleship Study* not only to convert non-Christians, but to bring to light the sharp Biblical distinction between the Lexington (later renamed Boston) Church of Christ, and all "other churches," including the Mainline Churches of Christ and the "Crossroads Ministries." As a result of the call to "total commitment" to God and the practice of the Biblical concept of discipleship from everyone in the congregation, the Boston Church of Christ multiplied disciples at an unprecedented rate!

Kip and Elena in front of what once was the
Lexington Church of Christ building
in 1979, but presently is
a Buddhist Temple!

Another of Kip's radical Biblical restorations was the role of an evangelist. He believed that the evangelist's charge was not simply to shepherd his congregation, but to evangelize that church's region of influence. (2 Corinthians 10:13-16) Thus in Boston, he divided the city into four geographical *"regions."* An evangelist was placed over the disciples that lived in this *"territory"* for the purpose of evangelizing the entire *"field."* In each region there were a number of "house churches," and in each house church there were a number of Bible Talks. This "pyramidal structure" was Kip's innovative application of Exodus 18:13-26.

To have the church appreciate the incredible training and sacrifice to become an Evangelist or Women's Ministry Leader, Kip and Elena began to appoint qualified individuals in front of the congregation. During this powerful ceremony, Kip (or Elena if appointing a Women's Ministry Leader) would share personally about the deserving disciple and then close out with the "ancient charge" of 2 Timothy 4:1-2 and the presentation of a Bible. This practice was imitated *"everywhere in every church"* in the Boston Movement, thus further unifying the churches. (1 Corinthians 4:14-17) So amazing is that every congregation in the Boston Movement "recognized" the appointed Evangelists and Women's Ministry Leaders throughout the other churches in the Movement!

# UNPRECEDENTED
# GROWTH AND IMPACT

During the ten years that the McKeans served the Lord in leading the Boston Church of Christ, the Spirit produced exponential growth! The original Lexington Church of Christ had witnessed only two baptisms in the previous three years before June 1, 1979. Through the restoration of the radical call and practice that every member of the congregation is "totally committed," the Boston Church of Christ had 103 baptisms the first year! The most dynamic Mainline Church of Christ for decades had only baptized 200 to 300 each year. In fact, during the 80's, every year a list of Mainline Churches of Christ baptizing 100 or more was published which usually had only 15 Mainline Churches listed. With God's Spirit working through the McKeans, the Boston Church of Christ saw exactly 200 baptisms their second year; 256 their third; 368 in the fourth; 457 in the fifth; 679 in the sixth; 735 in the seventh; 947 in the eighth; 1424 in the ninth; and in the Boston Church's tenth year 1621 were baptized into Christ. By this time also, the Sunday attendance in Boston was approaching 4,000 as the church met in the famed Boston Garden – "home" of the Boston Celtics professional basketball team. Not only was this the largest single congregation in the history of New England, but it also became the largest "Church of Christ" in the entire world!

Perhaps unappreciated by the casual observer was the challenge to meet the needs and keep faithful the unprecedented number of new Christians – over 2,000 in the first six years in Boston! In the 60's and 70's in the denominational world, there had been much discussion and writing on the "body life of the church" and "shepherding one another." Thus, in the Crossroads Movement, "one another Christianity" was expressed in a buddy system called "prayer partners," where each person chose their own "buddy" or "buddies." The idea was to spend one-on-one time sharing their lives and praying together. However, some chose Christians of the opposite sex, which in some cases led to sin!

In the McKeans' second year, the Lexington Church moved to the beautiful First Baptist Church of Arlington. (pictured above) Then in 1982, they began to meet in the Boston Opera House, so the Lexington Church changed their name to the Boston Church of Christ.

With so many new Christians in the Boston Church of Christ, Kip felt that the "buddy system" approach was not effective. Building upon the concepts of "shepherding" and "prayer partners," he came up with "discipleship partners." In these relationships, the evangelists, elders and women's ministry leaders – after discussion and prayer – arranged for an older or stronger Christian of the same sex to give direction to each of the younger or weaker ones. (This principle of mentoring is clearly seen in Jesus' relationship with the Twelve, as well as in Paul's relationships with Timothy and Titus. Again, this principle is taught in Titus 2:3-5, as the older women are commanded to train the younger women.) Each pair was expected to meet weekly and have daily contact. (Hebrews 3:12-13) This "one-over-one" discipling paradigm was also applied to marriages; thus came the innovation of "marriage discipling" – a mature married couple mentoring a younger married couple. Also honoring marriage, another of Kip's creative innovations was to replace "Bachelor Parties" (often accompanied with worldly overtones) with "Groom Honoring Parties." At these fun and moving events – very different from the world – bachelorhood was not mourned, rather marriage was honored!

# THE BOSTON MOVEMENT PLANTINGS

In 1981, the Lord put a vision on Kip's heart: "The evangelization of the nations in a generation." This passion was ignited as he was influenced by former missionaries and the mission efforts especially by the Sunset School of Preaching – a Mainline Church of Christ school that trained preachers – located in Lubbock, Texas. Kip's plan was a simple one: If the Boston Church of Christ could place a small group of disciples (a mission team) in each of the key metropolitan centers of the world, they in turn – by the multiplication of leaders and disciples – could send church plantings to each of the capital cities of the surrounding nations that were under their influence. Then these "capital city churches" could send out church plantings throughout that nation. Therefore, collectively, these capital city churches would evangelize the nations in one generation just as in the first century. (Acts 19:8-10; Colossians 1:6, 23)

The key churches planted in the major metropolitan centers were called "pillar churches" – for a world brotherhood was envisioned to be built on them. Dr. Donald McGavran, the "Father of Modern Church Growth" (in the broadest definition of Christianity), saw the Boston Movement as unique in that it had a plan to evangelize the entire world from one congregation. Almost everyone in the Boston Movement saw the uniqueness of this simple plan as God revealing "His plan" to "evangelize the nations in a generation."

Kip zealously pursued this vision, as he trained ministers in Boston. Women were also trained in "women's ministry" by Elena and Pat Gempel. These trained ministry couples were sent to the "pillar cities." In 1982, Chicago, Illinois and London, England, were the first two plantings of the Boston Movement. By the year 2000, the Chicago Church attendance was 5,000 and the London Church attendance was 3,000.

In 1983, the New York City Church of Christ was planted. Though this city had a population of 18 million, only 18 disciples were sent from Boston. Kip deeply believed that only one church of "totally committed" disciples – no matter how small – was all that was needed to evangelize an entire metropolitan area – no matter how large. At its zenith in 2001, the New York City Church had 7,000 in attendance.

In 1985, Toronto, Canada became the Boston Movement's second foreign planting. The Lord blessed this congregation with over 100 baptisms in their very first year!

In 1986, Johannesburg, South Africa was planted. God used this planting in a powerful way to glorify His name among the nations. Though Mainline Church of Christ preachers advised Kip to plant two churches in Johannesburg – a black church and a white church, Kip strove to honor God by sending one mission team, fully realizing that persecution laid ahead. The 22-member mission team – composed with an equal number of Caucasians and Blacks – became a powerful testimony to the lost worshipping together as one church! God in turn honored these faithful stands against Apartheid, as the laws of Apartheid in South Africa began to be struck down in 1990. Paris and Stockholm were also planted in 1986.

In 1987 came the plantings of Mexico City, Mexico; Buenos Aires, Argentina; and Hong Kong, China. Also, in 1987, came the milestone of the Boston Movement Churches abandoning autonomy to form one "world brotherhood" which would have a central leadership. This was detailed in three articles in the *LA Story* (the LA ICOC Bulletin) entitled: *Revolution*, *Multiplicity* and *From Here To Eternity*. These and many other articles articulated the unified stance that autonomy was the evil which would ensure that the world would never be evangelized, let alone in our generation.

In 1988, Bombay, India; Cairo, Egypt; and Tokyo, Japan were planted. The Tokyo planting was built on the Mainline Yoyogi-Hachiman Church of Christ foundation of the 1950's built by George and Irene Gurganus – whom Kip affectionately called his "Spiritual Grandparents." During this reconstruction in this very atheistic nation, Kip preached, "Where it is darkest the light shines brightest!"

In 1989, there were seven plantings whose mission teams were collectively composed of 120 Bible Talk Leaders sent out from Boston: Bangkok, Thailand; Honolulu, Hawaii; Los Angeles, California; Manila, Philippines; Miami/Ft. Lauderdale, Florida; Seattle, Washington; and Washington DC.

In 1990, the McKeans moved from Boston to Los Angeles to inspire the other church leaders of the Movement by leading a smaller church which was "more relatable in size" to the other Boston Movement congregations – thus more easily imitated. It was from Los Angeles in 1991 that Moscow, Russia was planted.

Valiantly, Kip and Elena personally led the mission teams to Manila, Bangkok and Moscow! In the first year in Manila, 400 were baptized into Christ! In Moscow's first year, an astounding 850 souls were baptized into Christ!

Kip's photo of the Moscow Mission Team on July 9, 1991 –
the day they landed in Moscow! (Elena is
pictured on the far right.)

Of note, in the summer of 1989 after planting Manila, Kip
courageously moved his family to Cairo after seven of the
original eight mission team members – who were Americans
– were deported by the government. This was a daring
decision for Kip, Elena and their three young children. Kip
felt that if he was to call others to preach in such life-
threatening places as the Middle East, he himself must set an
example to demonstrate this radical level of faith and
sacrifice. Not only in his six weeks where he valiantly led
the Cairo Church, but throughout all of his years in ministry
to this present day, there have been several death threats
against Kip and even a few against his whole family, as
preaching the truth always earns Satan's wrath. (Revelation
2:13, 12:17)

In 2011, the Egyptian lawyer John Beshai – a hero of the
evangelization of the Middle East – joined the SoldOut
Movement! John went home to the Father on
September 1, 2013.

Unique to the Boston Movement, not only did disciples
make disciples, but churches planted churches. The Boston
Church planted each of the "pillar churches," which planted
other churches, which planted still others. By 2001, at the
time of his sabbatical, there were almost 400 churches in 171
nations and a combined Sunday morning attendance of about
200,000! 42 churches had more than 1,000 in attendance and
15 churches had more than 3,000 in attendance! The largest
international congregation was the Manila Church at 6,000
in attendance! These numbers were staggering when
compared with the Mainline Churches of Christ or any
denominational group. Never in history has any church
growth movement ever spread as quickly and to so many
nations!

Through the 80's greatly aiding this expansion was the
coming into the Movement of more than 3,000 mostly young
people from the various elements of the Mainline Churches
of Christ, especially the "Crossroads Campus Ministry
Churches." They moved to Boston or to one of the Boston
Church of Christ plantings to become disciples or be
strengthened as disciples, and to train to be on mission

teams. These people – many of whom were leaders – were in awe of God and the unprecedented growth that the Holy Spirit produced in Boston and her daughter churches. They were often referred to as "remnant disciples." (Isaiah 10:20-22) Kip documents this exciting Biblical phenomenon of God gathering His remnant in both *Revolution Through Restoration Part I and Part II.*

In retrospect, one amazing aspect of this young movement was that many of these "remnant disciples" who were leaders had several philosophical and doctrinal conflicts with each other. However, Kip made every effort to forge a bond of unity between all of these leaders from the Scriptures by calling them to work side-by-side for one purpose. (Philippians 1:27; 2:1-4) Over time being *"partners in the Gospel"* helped them to surrender their personal perspectives and be united in pursuing "the dream!"

On a sad note in 1987, the Crossroads Church of Christ sinfully "disfellowshipped" the McKeans, the Boston Church of Christ, and all of its affiliated plantings. This occurred after the Atlanta Church of the Boston Movement was "planted" through a split of the Sandy Springs Church of Christ – a "Crossroads Ministry Congregation." The Board of Directors of the Sandy Springs Church wanted to remain autonomous, and so did not want to join the Boston Movement. However, Sam Laing and the rest of the full-time ministry staff – believing that they were the true spiritual leaders of the church – were wholehearted in this decision to call every member to be "totally committed" and join what they saw as God's Movement. Therefore, the congregation split over whether to follow the laws of the land versus obeying the men of God. At this historic juncture and without debate, this made a clear distinction between the Boston Movement and what was left of the Crossroads Movement, which was in sharp decline beginning in 1985 after the departure from the full-time ministry of their leader Chuck Lucas for personal reasons. It must be noted that after the Crossroads elders made the decision to disfellowship the

Boston Movement, almost immediately two full-time ministers at Crossroads resigned and moved to Boston.

# CENTRAL LEADERSHIP: THE WORLD SECTOR LEADERS

In 1988, because of the rapid expanse of the churches, several brothers encouraged Kip to focus on a few *"capable... and trustworthy men."* (Exodus 18:13-26) After six months of prayerful consideration and several discussions, Kip and Elena chose nine couples: Doug and Joyce Arthur, Al and Gloria Baird, Tom and Kelly Brown, Bob and Pat Gempel, Scott and Lynne Green, Steve and Lisa Johnson, Frank and Erica Kim, Phil and Donna Lamb, and Randy and Kay McKean. These leaders – whom the McKeans had personally trained for the ministry – Kip called "World Sector Leaders."

The World Sector Leaders in 1992 – Front Row: Bob Gempel, Kip McKean, Phil Lamb and Al Baird. Second Row: Marty Fuqua, Scott Green, Doug Arthur, Randy McKean, Steve Johnson and Frank Kim.

This was extremely significant because the Mainline Church of Christ believes in autonomy – the independence of each congregation. Practically, autonomy means that all final decisions about that local congregation are made by the local leadership. They believe that conferring with leaders from other congregations is good, but there is no overseeing authority, which can give directives on matters such as: dealing with difficult situations, raising and sending money for mission efforts, or calling for certain disciples for mission teams to complete an overall plan. Yet in the Scriptures, Paul wrote the "overseeing evangelist" Titus (who Paul himself oversaw), *"The reason I left you in Crete was that you might straighten out what was left unfinished and appoint elders in every town, as I directed you... for there are many rebellious people, mere talkers and deceivers... They must be silenced... Therefore, encourage and rebuke with all authority."* (Titus 1:5, 10-11; 2:15) So Kip and Elena, because of their vision and convictions from Scriptures, forged a "leadership family" where each couple would "oversee" the evangelization of "their region" of the world – a World Sector. Collectively these World Sectors covered the globe!

In 1988, since there now existed a formal central leadership in Boston – the World Sector Leaders with a central leader (Kip), it was at this point that most Mainline Churches of Christ either distanced themselves or disfellowshipped Kip and the Boston Movement Churches. They saw a central leader as a "Pope" and thus in their minds unscriptural, like the Catholic Church.

Of note, during the first few years of the World Sector Leaders, the McKeans alongside the Bairds and the Gempels – as Shepherding Couples – would make the major decisions for the Movement. Later, the Arthurs, the Kims and the Johnsons were added to this decision-making group.

On January 1, 1990, the McKeans went to fortify the Los Angeles Church, which was planted in August 1989 by Tom and Kelly Brown. In turn, the Browns were sent back to Boston for strengthening, and Marty and Chris Fuqua replaced them as World Sector Leaders. When the McKeans arrived, the Los Angeles Church had 154 members. By March 1993 when I was baptized, church services were incredible celebrations of God's glory! At that time, the LA

Church was having 3,000 in attendance! Amazingly in 2001, the last year that the McKeans led the congregation, there were 10,000 members with about 15,000 in attendance regularly every Sunday morning, and 2,500 were baptized that year! Of special note, one of my most memorable worship services of the LA ICOC was when 17,000 of us gathered on a warm Saturday evening in November 8, 1997 in one of America's largest stadiums – the Rose Bowl! At this glorious occasion, Kip's visionary sermon was simply entitled, The Purposes Of God.

As well in 1991, the McKeans asked Bob and Pat Gempel to become the Directors of the newly founded HOPE*worldwide* as their charge as World Sector Leaders. HOPE*worldwide* was created to be the "benevolent arm" of the Boston Movement Churches. Its uniqueness from all other charity organizations was that the World Sector Leaders could mobilize every member of every church in every country for a focused volunteer effort to help the poor and needy around the world.

Kip and Elena and Bob and Pat Gempel – at this time
the McKeans' closest friends – strolled through
the Garden of Gethsemane in 1994.

In 1994, the World Sector Leaders of the Boston Movement officially adopted the name International Church of Christ (ICOC). This name was first given to the Boston Movement by John Vaughn, a denominational church growth expert. He surmised that the vast majority of the Mainline Churches of Christ were located in the "Bible Belt" of America, but the Boston Movement (to him with a slightly different plan of salvation, which included becoming a disciple in order to be baptized) had an equal number of congregations internationally as they did nationally. So, in his articles from his research, he distinguished between the Mainline Churches of Christ and the Boston Movement Churches, thus birthing the name: "International" Churches of Christ!

The World Sector Leaders in the Fall of 1994. By this time, Cory and Megan Blackwell had been added to the group to spearhead the evangelization of the Middle East!

Also, in 1994, Kip wrote and laid out his most visionary project to date – *The Evangelization Proclamation!* Signed first by the McKeans and then by all the World Sector Leader Men and Women, they vowed before God to plant a discipling church in every nation of the world that had a city with at least a population of 100,000 by the end of the year 2000! *The Evangelization Proclamation* read:

51

*On this fourth day of February, in the year of Our Lord one thousand nine hundred and ninety-four, we the World Sector Leaders issue this proclamation:*

*We place before each true disciple the unanswered and most ancient of Christian challenges: The completion of the Great Commission. We affirm and assert that Jesus' last command to the eleven faithful disciples was to evangelize the world in their generation. Obeyed by the Apostles, this guiding command extends to each succeeding generation, yet has not been accomplished again for almost two millennia. As God's modern-day Movement, the time is now for each true disciple to go far beyond any feats of faith or deeds of daring witnessed to this hour. In this proclamation we issue such a challenge.*

*"Miracle" is the defining word of the decade and a half since our attack against the darkness was launched. In Boston scarcely more than fourteen years ago, 30 would-be disciples gathered in the living room of Bob and Pat Gempel. They came together bonded by the blood of Jesus, the Spirit of our God, the Bible as the only inspired and inerrant Scriptures and a conviction that only the totally committed could be members of the Lexington Church of Christ (later renamed Boston). In the next few months the Bible doctrine from Acts 11:26 of Saved = Christian = Disciple was crystallized. The Spirit then gave us a deep conviction that only these baptized disciples comprise God's Kingdom on earth. This was and still is the true church of Jesus.*

*Thirteen years ago prompted by the Holy Spirit, the elders and evangelists of the Boston Church of Christ made the radical decision that young men and women who desired to be leaders in the church should be trained in a local congregation, not in a seminary. We also believed that because of doctrinal and lifestyle differences we could not in good conscience send our young, newly trained leaders into existing Mainline Churches.*

52

*Twelve years ago, we embarked on an historic revolutionary path to send mission teams of disciples from Boston into the world's largest and most influential cities. We called the churches planted in these cities "pillar churches" because they would become the principal supports for an international brotherhood and in turn would evangelize the capital cities of the nations in their regions of influence. The capital city churches would then evangelize all the cities and villages of their nations. With this dream and our prayers, God moved with the twin church plantings of Chicago and London.*

*Eleven years ago, God's hand touched New York City. Though this city of darkness had a population of 18 million in the metropolitan area, only 18 disciples were sent from Boston. We believed only one church of disciples, no matter how small, would be sufficient for God to use them to saturate the city with his Word if they remained faithful to the command to make disciples who made disciples who made disciples. This radical doctrine [of one church, one city] was confirmed in Scripture by example: Jerusalem, Ephesus, Smyrna, Pergamum, Thyatira, Sardis, Philadelphia, Laodicea, and the great metropolis of Rome had only one church.*

*Ten years ago, a remnant of disciples from various Churches of Christ, Christian Churches and other denominational movements left everything and moved to Boston or our plantings. We were widely labeled the "Boston Movement." Eight years ago a miracle happened in Johannesburg, where in the church blacks and whites did not merely coexist, but for the first time hugged one another in the midst of apartheid and under the threat of extremists. Paris and Stockholm were also miracle churches which proved language an inconsequential barrier to the preaching of the cross.*

*Seven years ago came the first reconstructions. At the request of leaders in Mainline Churches, the elders and*

53

*evangelists of the Boston Church sent trained preachers into these congregations to call out more of the remnant. Revolutionary, Nehemiah-like sermons were delivered to these existing Mainline Churches, and those individuals who responded by renewing their initial disciple's commitment or were baptized as disciples formed new congregations that were now no different from the other Boston Movement Churches. Each was composed solely of baptized disciples. Kingston and Sydney were the first of some twenty reconstructed churches. Also, at this time was the miracle of Bombay where God began to annihilate the demons of poverty, disease and apathy. Now, seven churches minister to the almost one billion people of India. HOPEworldwide was formed to become the benevolent arm of our brotherhood.*

*Six years ago came the plantings of Mexico City, Hong Kong and Cairo. After many months of study, counsel, and a final all night of prayer, the World Sector Leaders were selected. The nations of the world were divided into sectors, and each World Sector Leader Couple was given a charge to evangelize their sector in this generation.*

*Five years ago, Manila, Tokyo and Los Angeles began. Literally thousands, as in the Book of Acts, were baptized in these three cities giving us the vision of super-churches in each of the metropolitan cities of the world. The Los Angeles Church now has an attendance of 6,000 on Sundays.*

*Four years ago, an attack was launched on Satan's throne in Bangkok where one in six women is engaged in prostitution, and AIDS is clearly becoming the Black Death of the Nineties.*

*Three short years ago, God melted the Iron Curtain. The Moscow Church of Christ was planted and already has over 2,000 in attendance, and five daughter churches in the Commonwealth of Independent States.*

54

*Two years ago, came the first fifth-generation church: Boston planted London, London planted Sydney, Sydney planted Auckland and Auckland planted God 's church in the Cook Islands. Less than one year ago at the World Missions Leadership Conference, all the evangelists, women's ministry leaders, and elders in all of our churches gathered in the Los Angeles Sports Arena along with 10,000 other disciples as we formally adopted the name "International Churches of Christ." God in His grace and mercy has blessed His modern-day Movement of true Christians as our churches now number 146 with an attendance of over 75,000! True churches are now established in 53 of the 216 nations of the world. Today compelled by the Spirit and five billion lost souls, we lay before the brotherhood a simple but comprehensive strategy for the completion of world evangelism. Presently, there exist 160 countries with a city of at least 100,000 people. Disciples are in only 49. Therefore, in the presence of God and Christ Jesus who will judge the living and the dead and in view of His appearing and His Kingdom we give you this charge: Give to God your dreams, energies, health, finances, intellects, families, and yes, even your life, to plant churches in the remaining 111 nations by the year 2000. Let us reach the remaining small, unevangelized nations early in the next millennium. To make possible the evangelization of all nations, an historic financial plan has been instituted. No longer will it be the sole responsibility of American Churches to finance missions, but all first-world churches will join together to take up a yearly missions collection that will be used to finance new and existing third-world churches. This allows the Kingdom to make more rapid progress with the difficult third-world plantings. The second-world churches will likewise give a missions contribution which will allow them to become self-supporting and evangelize their respective nations. Since the first-world finances will only manage to initiate third-world plantings, the third-world churches must also sacrifice in unprecedented ways to contribute toward their own mission works even to the point of some of these churches being led by unpaid disciples. For these dreams to become reality, nationals must ready themselves now to return to their homelands. Of ultimate necessity for all of us is fervent prayer unseen in our day. Only zealous prayer will allow God to empower, embolden and employ each of us to fulfill our individual destiny, and thus this global proclamation.*

*Though unprecedented, our past efforts are but a flickering flame in a universe of demonic darkness. If we are to change the course of human events, we must remember that like all flesh our time on earth is but a mist. The tombs of Mohammed, Buddha, Confucius, Lincoln, Lenin and Gandhi are but dust and darkness. Like the faithful Eleven our overriding inspiration lies in the empty, light-filled tomb of Jesus. This is our one and only sure hope – eternal life. To complete the commission, all of the Eleven but John died a martyr's death – this was and still is the ultimate price for world evangelism. Therefore, let us go forth together with a resolve that even the gates of hell will not prevail. Only heaven awaits. And to God be the glory!\*\**

*\*\* The longer quotes from Kip are highlighted in azure blue.*

*The Evangelization Proclamation* became more commonly known as *The Six Year Plan*. At its signing, we were in "just" 53 countries. Through the power of God, this monumental task was accomplished by July 2000! Unprecedented in the history of Christianity, in just 21 years, God had multiplied the "30 would-be disciples" in the Boston Church to almost 400 churches, 135,000 disciples in 171 nations with a combined Sunday attendance of 200,000!

The Women World Sector Leaders in 1998 – First Row:
Chris Fuqua, Megan Blackwell, Gloria Baird, Elena
McKean, Pat Gempel and Kay McKean. Second
Row: Donna Lamb, Erika Kim, Lisa Johnson,
Joyce Arthur and Lynne Green.

Very encouraging to the Movement were the following
leadership appointments. In the late 80's, Kip asked Cecil
Wooten – a two-time recipient of the Purple Heart in World
War II and the former Vice President of Chicago Bridge and
Iron – to become the Administrator of the Boston Movement
Churches. Each World Sector Leader had a World Sector
Administrator. Cecil oversaw and coordinated this group. In
1993, the McKeans asked Al and Gloria Baird to oversee a
new world sector called the "Media and Law World Sector."
Also at that time, the McKeans trained Cory Blackwell – a
former NBA basketball player – and his wife Megan for the
ministry, while initiating the "Cross and Switchblade
Ministry" in the dangerous neighborhoods of South Central
LA. Since Cory's single mother was a devote Muslim, the
Blackwells were asked by the McKeans to become the
World Sector Leaders for the Middle East. (Cory's mom –
Wazirah – was later baptized in 1999!)

Wazirah, Cory Blackwell's mother, fellowshipping in
2013 with Elena, whom Cory affectionately
calls his "spiritual mom."

Another replacement among the World Sector Leaders was
made when the Lambs, because of "family and health
issues," were asked to step aside in order to receive
strengthening. (Sadly, the Lambs later divorced. Phil fell
away, yet Donna remained faithful till her death by cancer in
December 2007.) To replace the Lambs, who oversaw the
Central and South America World Sector, Peter and Laura
Garcia-Bengochea – the trusted brother and sister-in-law of
Elena – were asked to serve in this role. In 1999, Cecil was
in his 70's and wanted to take a step back from the rigorous
demands of administration. Consequently, Andy and
Tammy Fleming were selected to assume his role as the
leaders of all the administrators throughout the ICOC. The
McKeans made this into the "Administration World Sector."
The last World Sector Leaders selected were Russ and Gail
Ewell. They led the "NET World Sector" – New media,
Exceptional children, and Technology.

The leadership structure of the International Churches of
Christ was as simple as it was creative and unique. Of the
original World Sector Leaders – except the Gempels and the
Bairds whose role was to shepherd the group – each was

given a geographic charge. There evolved eight geographic World Sectors: British Commonwealth – Great Britain, India, Singapore, Indonesia, and Australia (Arthurs); ACES – Africa, Caribbean, Eastern States (Johnsons); Europe (the Randy McKeans); Pacific Rim (Kims); Central and South America (Lambs); Northern Federation – former Soviet Union nations; Scandinavia, Canada and the Western US (Fuquas); China (Greens); and later the Middle East (Blackwells). Each World Sector Leader Couple's discipling group was composed of 10-12 other couples: a World Sector Administrator, a World Sector Elder, a World Sector Teacher, and Geographic Sector Leaders (Evangelists and Women's Ministry Leaders). Also, in most world sectors, there was a World Sector Media and Law Couple. The World Sector Elders were collectively called the "Kingdom Elders." They were overseen by the Bairds. The Teachers in each World Sector were collectively known as the "Kingdom Teachers," and were eventually led by Andy Fleming. The Geographic Sector Leaders (GSL) oversaw the evangelism of a region of that World Sector. For example, in the ACES, Mike and Anne-Brigitte Taliaferro were the "GSL Couple" for Africa, and in the Northern Federation, Sasha and Louisa Kostenko served as the "GSL Couple" for the 15 nations in the former Soviet Union – the Commonwealth of Independent States. In time, each GSL Couple built their own discipleship group, which was composed of essentially an evangelist and women's ministry leader for each nation or group of nations, which was in their geographic charge.

# WORLD MISSIONS EVANGELIST SABBATICAL

At the beginning of 2001 as a college student in Boston, the oldest of the McKeans' children began to question her faith. Though everyone who falls away must take full responsibility for this decision, it must be noted that this young woman was unjustly and heavily criticized – largely because of the high profile and jealousy of her parents. This feeling of being unloved by key leaders in the congregation contributed to her no longer attending church in April 2001. (Luke 17:1-2) This single event caused uncertainty in the McKeans' leadership among many of the World Sector Leaders, as well as among the Kingdom Elders and Kingdom Teachers. So, in September of 2001, the World Sector Leaders "compelled" the McKeans to go on sabbatical – though later, some deeply regretted this decision.

Upon the McKeans' daughter falling away, 1 Timothy 3:4-5 was presented to the McKeans to step down from leadership, *"[An overseer] must manager his own family well and see that his children obey him with proper respect. If anyone does not know how to manage his own family, how can he take care of God's church?"* Cited incorrectly to Kip and Elena was Proverbs 22:6, *"Train a child in the way he should go, and… he will not turn from it."* Left out from this quote is the phrase, *"when he is old."* Disregarding what is obviously implied in the phrase *"when he is old,"* is that during their younger years children may not be faithful to God, but will return to the Kingdom because of their good training when they are *"old."* (This has now been seen in the SoldOut Movement and the ICOC over and over again.) Even sadder is the lack of grace by almost all of the World Sector Leaders, Kingdom Elders and Kingdom Teachers. In the Scriptures, some of God's greatest leaders had unfaithful children – Aaron, Samuel, and even the Old Testament's *"man after God's own heart,"* David – yet they continued to victoriously lead "all Israel."

60

Kip was profoundly affected by his beloved daughter leaving the faith, the "stripping away" of his leadership, and the public condemnation by some of the most prominent ICOC leaders of his "leadership style," and the Biblical teachings that propelled the movement to almost all nations. Most of all, he was brokenhearted at the decimation of the churches that came in early 2003. I remember quite vividly those dark days of the McKeans' sabbatical.

One factor in my decision to wholeheartedly follow Kip as God's man – even though he was not my direct father in the faith – was through my experiences as the "IT contractor" for the LA ICOC in 2002. Along with moving all of the servers and workstations from the old Normandie Avenue office to the Western Avenue office, my agreement included installing wireless devices on all of the LA ICOC ministers' computers. During this process, I was asked by virtually every LA minister to purchase additional wireless devices for their children's computers and to add it to "my bill to the church." To my recollection the only exception was Kip. Yes, he asked me to help with his children's computers. However, to my surprise, he then paid me separately for the devices and the work to install them on their computers. Even though I was drifting in my walk with Christ without discipling, seeing Kip's integrity reminded me not only of "what was right," but later would guide me to who was right.

After working on Elena's computer in that same year, I came downstairs to see my devastated friend and leader, distraught by the condition of God's family and hurting from the lost relationships of those who abandoned him in his time of need. The only words I could muster were, "Kip, I don't know what to say to you. But I do know that the whole Kingdom worldwide is falling apart around us and you need to 'get back on the horse.'" Through God's strength found in weakness, this he did!

In the past 15 years in both sermons and his writings, Kip is quite vulnerable about wrestling with bitterness, being

61

depressed and unmotivated, as well as drifting and becoming quite distant in his walk with God for about a year of this one-and-a-half year sabbatical. Kip has openly confessed that these were all signs of one of the rarely acknowledged "seven deadly sins" – "acedia," from which most other remnant disciples have suffered the consequences. (2 Corinthians 7:10; Hebrews 12:3, 15)

Kip's humble self-reflection and in-depth search of the Scriptures with a historical perspective created an exemplory article on acedia!

Kip wrote about "acedia" in the *June 2014 City of Angels Church Bulletin* entitled, *Acedia – The Forgotten Sin*:

*The word "acedia" has been lost to the modern English language and is the forgotten of the original "Seven Deadly Sins." Though acedia is not explicitly named on the many lists of sins in the Bible (Proverbs 6:16-19; 1*

Corinthians 6:9-10; Galatians 5:19-21; 2 Timothy 3:1-5), a monk named Evagrius Ponticus (345 – 399AD), one of the most gifted intellects of his day, compiled in Greek from Scripture his list of the "Eight Evil Thoughts." In this order Ponticus included: gluttony (gastrimargia), fornication (porneia), avarice (philargyria), hubris (hyperephania), sadness – sadness at another's good fortune (lype), wrath (orge), boasting (kenodoxia), and acedia (akedia). Acedia is listed last because Ponticus considered it "the most troublesome of all."

A short time later, another celebrated monk John Cassian (360 – 435AD), translates Ponticus' list into Latin but with slight variances of meanings. Cassian's "Eight Evil Thoughts List" is: gluttony (gula), fornication (fornicatio), avarice (avaritia), pride (superbia), despair (tristitia), wrath (ira), vainglory (vaingloria), and acedia (acedia).

Then almost 200 years later, Gregorius Anicius (540 – 604AD) – the pope known as "Gregory the Great" and called by the Protestant Reformer John Calvin "the last good pope" – compiles a list of sins derived from Cassian's list which Anicius calls "The Seven Deadlies." In every day terms, Anicius combines pride and vainglory as well as despair and acedia, and then adds envy. Interestingly, he "changes" fornicatio (fornication) to "luxuria" – which expands the meaning from illicit sex to intense desire... lust! In Anicius' mind, this could be lust for power, food, drink, knowledge, money, and/or fame. Therefore, in English, the very first list of "The Seven Deadly Sins" is: lust, gluttony, greed, acedia, wrath, envy and pride.

Over the centuries the word "acedia" has been transliterated into "sloth" on most "Seven Deadly Sin Lists," not to mention "dropped from daily use" in the English language. But what is the definition of acedia – this once so "prominent of sins?" The Oxford Concise

*Dictionary of the Christian Church reads, "A state of restlessness and inability either to work or to pray." According to Wikipedia, "Acedia is the neglect to take care of something that one should do. It is [best] translated apathetic listlessness; depression without joy... In early Christian thought, the lack of joy was regarded as a willful refusal to enjoy the goodness of God and the world God created."*

*The respected theologian Thomas Aquinas (1225 – 1274AD) believed that acedia was that which Paul refers to in 2 Corinthians 7:10 as "worldly sorrow." Dante Alighieri (1265 – 1321AD), the prolific Italian writer of The Divine Comedy, calls acedia "the failure to love God with all one's heart, all one's mind, and all one's soul." The seriousness of this sin is underlined by the fact that for centuries many writers have expressed that acedia's ultimate manifestation is a "despair which leads to suicide."*

*As for me, acedia was not part of my vocabulary until I stumbled on this archaic word while casually researching "The Seven Deadly Sins." Immediately when I read about its earlier definitions, my heart was stirred because I – for the very first time – could identify my feelings and spiritual condition from 2001 – 2003AD. These were the years that I was put on sabbatical (taken out of all leadership and influence) and then fired for my convictions about the Scriptures (2 Timothy 3:16- 17); about the Biblical mandate of a central leadership with a central leader for God's people (Numbers 27:15-18; Judges 2:6-19); that discipling is a command of God for every Christian (Matthew 28:20); that the "visible church" is to be composed of only sold-out disciples (Acts 2:41-42); and that we as God's people are commanded to evangelize the nations in our generation. (1Timothy 2:3- 4)*

*After reading what others had written about acedia, I too begin to search the Scriptures. For me, Proverbs 13:12 sums it up best, "Hope deferred makes the heart sick, but a longing fulfilled is a tree of life." In 1 Corinthians 11, Paul teaches that when one is not regularly inspired by the "body and blood of Jesus" during communion that this is the reason "people in the church" are "weak, sick... and [have] fallen asleep." (1 Corinthians 11:30) The state of being "weak" most disciples comprehend, and "fallen asleep" of course means one has fallen away but still attends church. Yet, "spiritual sickness" is a term rarely used but it "fits" acedia!*

*Perhaps from these two passages one begins to understand why "sloth" in time was substituted for "acedia." When one is physically sick, one is usually lethargic – "hurting" and thus unmotivated "to get out of bed." So it is with "spiritual sickness" – one's heart is hurting so badly that one "feels" that it's just too hard "to get out of bed" to do the will of God. Sloth on the other hand is simply laziness – one "loves doing nothing" more than working for God. Acedia and sloth may look the same – no work done for God – but in fact they are very distinct. This seemly subtle substitution on The Seven Deadly Sins List may have been the beginning of Satan's scheme "to hide" the Biblical concept of acedia from our day and age.*

*So what is the cause of the forgotten sin of acedia – "spiritual sickness?" I believe it is bitterness in one's soul. In Hebrews 12 the Spirit says, "Endure [all] hardship as discipline [from] God." Since God is sovereign then everything that happens to us either God makes happen or He allows it. The Spirit says that "yes" this "discipline is painful," but God's purpose is to "produce a harvest of righteousness and peace..." So when hardship comes one has a choice either to become a "better Christian" or a "bitter Christian!" In other words, one "gets down and depressed" because one's life*

65

is not going as they had "hoped." Your hope is "deferred!" This is why Hebrews 12:15 teaches, "See to it that no one misses the grace of God and that no bitter root grows up to cause trouble and defile many." Many of us "picture" bitterness as a raging, hateful and loud individual. However, actually for most, bitterness makes us depressed, lethargic and withdrawn... just like Cain whose "face was downcast." (Genesis 4:6)

As I studied out this sin, I knew that I must look at the life of Jesus because He was "tempted in every way just as we are yet was without sin." (Hebrews 4:15) In Jesus' darkest hours in Gethsemane, He shares with His three closest brothers – Peter, James and John, "My soul is overwhelmed with sorrow to the point of death. Stay here and keep watch with me." (Matthew 26:38) Then He fell to the ground praying for three hours, "Father if it is possible, may this cup be taken from me. Yet not as I will, but as you will." (Matthew 26:39) Luke adds that His prayer was so intense that Jesus sweat drops of blood. Then Luke continues, "When Jesus rose from prayer and went back to the disciples, He found them asleep, exhausted from sorrow. 'Why are you sleeping?' Jesus asked them. 'Get up and pray so that you will not fall into temptation.'" (Luke 22:45-46) Most notably, Jesus is tempted with acedia and overcomes through prayer and surrendering His will to God's, but His disciples succumb to acedia – "exhausted from sorrow" – failing to even pray!

So, in retrospect in examining my own life, I was deceived by my sin and Satan. (Hebrews 3:12) Since I was a "happy pagan" before I was baptized; a "happy" young Christian; a "happy" Evangelist; and a "very happy" husband and father, when great adversity came, my heart was not like Jesus "who for the joy set before Him endured the cross." (Hebrews 12:2) When I faced "opposition from sinful men" (some I caused by my sin against them) I grew "weary and began to lose heart."

*(Hebrews 12:3) I did not "see God" anywhere in my hardship but I was bitter towards those that I perceived "hurt my family and me." Confused by Satan through the sin of acedia, I almost lost my ideals, my Biblical convictions, and my salvation. (John 8:43-44) Praise God that the Scriptures reveal "the truth, and the truth... set me free!" (John 8:32)*

*However, some nights... I still struggle with acedia – **"exhausted with sorrow."** In fact, I was recently convicted by the Disney movie FROZEN. I had a dream where Elena & I were sitting in a plane and watching other passengers board. Then two "brothers" (who in my opinion) did my family and me **"a great deal of harm"** came down the aisle. (2 Timothy 4:14) When the first one came to me, I immediately stood up and angrily rebuked him! When the second one passed, I was even more sinful! I said absolutely nothing as I scornfully watched him pass by. I told Elena the dream in the morning and I knew I needed to repent of this bitterness that had crept back into my heart. Then a few days later, I received an email informing me that the man to whom I had said nothing had just lost a son to cancer. Elena asked if I was going to write a sympathy note... She asked three days straight! I then cried when I saw that my heart was "FROZEN!" In the movie, the only cure for a "frozen heart" is "an act of true love." Remarkably, after I wrote and sent a warm email to this brother, I felt a peace come over me as my heart "melted" from this "act of love." I learned that I have to "re-crucify" my bitterness and reaffirm my forgiveness, especially since none was ever asked.*

*I write these things to help any others who can identify with me. Through God's incredible mercy and patience, I now see clearly that God had to take away everything that I valued too much. Like Nebuchadnezzar – who was **"driven away from people and ate grass like cattle"** – God greatly humbled me (except for eating grass) making me understand that I am nothing. (Daniel 4:33) Through*

67

*the **"hardship"** of losing all my leadership and most of my "friends," I learned that I must live only to praise **"the Most High!"** (Daniel 4:34) I thank God for Elena whose fierce loyalty and love pointed me to God and gave me strength to persevere.*

*I do believe that for most "remnant veteran disciples," acedia is our "sin of choice" as our **"hope"** of a glorious church that would reach all nations was **"deferred"** by our sins! How do we repent of acedia − "the most troublesome of sins?" First of all, you must identify it in your life. Secondly, you must surrender to the sovereignty of God, embracing your hardships by asking what God wants you to learn.*

*I still remember quite vividly studying with Carlos Mejia at the Good Earth Restaurant after he visited the Inaugural Service of the City of Angels Church in May 2007. At that time he shared that he was "visiting and checking out" many different churches and could not commit to any because he was "so sad" about the demise of our former fellowship and "how he was treated." Perhaps the most impacting Scripture for him was Luke 5:31-32, **"Jesus answered them, 'It is not the healthy who need a doctor, but the sick. I have not come to call the righteous but sinners to repentance.'"** I shared with Carlos from this passage that to be **"sick"** is to be a **"sinner"** and that **"repentance"** makes us **"healthy."** In response, Carlos repented of his acedia − spiritual sickness − that day and placed membership the next Sunday! But now when Carlos shares about that Sunday, he simply says, "I was restored to my first love!" Furthermore, today Carlos powerfully leads the Santiago de Chile International Christian Church! Be sure of this, "healing" from this sin is not a matter of time but **"repentance!"** Then as part of your **"repentance"** of bitterness, forgive those who have hurt you or you will not be forgiven. (Matthew 18:23-35)*

*Since acedia is "the wilful refusal to enjoy the goodness of God" be aware that this sin will return with his seven deadly demon friends unless you wilfully **"rejoice in the Lord always... [and pray] with thanksgiving... [so that] the peace of God which transcends all understanding will guard your hearts and minds in Christ Jesus... [Therefore] whatever is true, whatever is noble, whatever is right, whatever is pure, whatever is lovely, whatever is admirable – if anything is excellent or praiseworthy – think about such things... [Remembering you] can do everything through Him who gives [you] strength!"** (Philippians 4:4-13) Even overcoming acedia! And to our Merciful Father in Heaven be all the glory!*

In 2002, in Manila, even in the midst of painful attacks on his character and family, the Lord allowed Kip to continue to preach the Word, where he was still acknowledged as the "father of faith."

*The Acedia – The Forgotten Sin* article is one of the most widely distributed *CAICC Bulletin Articles.* It is Kips' conviction that almost all remnant disciples suffer from some form of this "most troublesome of all" sins from the traumatic events around the collapse of the ICOC.

In the summer of 2002, the McKeans were invited to Bald Head Island, North Carolina, which is located near where the Cape Fear River empties into the Atlantic. There Kip spent hours alone wrestling with God to overcome acedia. Kip wrote the following as recorded in *Revolution Through Restoration – Part III*:

> *In the waters off the beach known as Cape Fear, there were huge, raging waves as the currents of the Atlantic Ocean collided with the currents of the Cape Fear River. Historically, this tumult resulted in many shipwrecks. I went to spend time with God at Cape Fear. I soon noticed that where there should have been a lighthouse, there was only a weathered foundation. This is what I wrote that day:*
>
> ### THE CAPE FEAR PSALM
> *The rage of the opposing currents*
> *Has shipwrecked my faith.*
> *The lighthouse has gone*
> *And I have no direction.*
> *I am alone for I feel your anger Lord*
> *From your Word and from people who feel like foes,*
> *That used to call me friend and leader.*
> *I gloried in your victories*
> *Which I foolishly called my own*
>
> *And now your hand is pushing me under the currents*
> *For I exalted myself, and not your grace.*
> *I am weary through unceasing pain*
> *From morning until night,*
> *In sleep there is a peace when I close my eyes.*
> *But my dreams are full of anguish and darkness.*
> *Because your lighthouse has been destroyed.*
>
> *I am drowning in self-pity and bitterness engulfs me.*
> *You know that I cannot bear much more.*

*I fear for your Movement.*
*I fear for my family.*
*And I fear most for my soul.*
*I have thoughts of dying*
*But realize there would await me*
*Only an unrelenting, malicious presence,*
*To be eternally away from you.*

*My daily tears have been for me,*
*Yet now they are because I have disappointed you*
*And have hurt so many through my sins.*
*Please forgive my arrogance.*
*I became confused in my pride*
*And I turned from your wisdom to mine.*
*I stopped consulting your Word and my brother*
*prophets.*

*Let my heart return to that simple eternal moment*
*Where I first saw your lighthouse.*
*Through the calm sea of baptism*
*I responded to your Word.*
*I first felt your Fatherly embrace*
*Just 30 short years ago.*

*I was indignant at your enemies of false prophets*
*Those hypocritical leaders of your people*
*For they led me and the whole world astray.*
*I was damaged by their arrogance and sin.*

*But by your Mighty Hand, even that first day*
*You gave me the strength to confront them.*
*Now I am them. I find no fellowship*
*Only angry confrontations.*
*The prophets I trained are furious*
*At the damage I have caused your movement.*
*Few remember my deeds, fewer my zeal,*
*Only you know my heart.*

*Father, lead me to rebuild that lighthouse.*
*If your mercy allows, I will help to rebuild it.*

*Today I promise you I will stop drifting out to sea.*
*Today I promise I will swim till I reach the other shore.*
*I will not quit.*

*I realize my sacrifice*
*Only brought you ever-lessening pleasure,*
*As my heart became dull.*
*For you desire only a broken and contrite heart.*
*Only these prayers are the incense of Heaven.*

*Today I promise to strive to be only a disciple.*
*I surrender my ambition to lead*
*Till you refine it in the fires of criticism.*
*I will no longer care what the media, my enemies*
*And even my friends say.*
*Because this brought me to Cape Fear.*
*Only your approval will I seek.*

*My most heartfelt prayer is*
*Let me and my family make it through the raging*
*currents.*
*Let your lighthouse shine mightily*
*So we can make it to the other side.*

Kip continued in *Revolution Through Restoration – Part III* reflecting on how his sins affected the Movement:

*During the sabbatical, God taught me to take responsibility for my leadership in the Movement, the decisions of the World Sector Leaders, and for the spiritual condition of each person in my family. My sins are clear and grievous. I have been arrogant, almost always thinking I was right. I did not listen. I did not actively seek discipling for me and my family. I was only partially open and deceit came into my life. This led to the sin of anger towards those who disagreed with me. Too often, I viewed these individuals as critical. I did not draw people out. I built an atmosphere in which people were afraid to speak up. There were times when I corrected people that I was mean, cruel and I even humiliated them.*

72

*I was too controlling. For this I apologize. I am truly sorry...*

*Ultimately, my most devastating sin was claiming God's victories as mine. In pride, I boasted in "my" accomplishments. I allowed people to give me glory; I did not refocus them to God. Though some have charged "growth was god," this was never true. My goal was, and still is, simply **"to win as many as possible."** (1 Corinthians 9:19) However, people developed wrong motivations and stumbled because of my overemphasis on numeric goals and accountability, though I still believe in accountability if it is used wisely as Jesus did. (Mark 6:30) In retrospect, I see that many leaders did not imitate Christ in me, but my ungodly leadership traits, and they are now being hurt by those they hurt. I confessed these sins while sharing my sabbatical journey at the Unity Meeting in LA [specifically Long Beach] in November 2002.*

One evangelist called the *Cape Fear Psalm*, "Kip's Psalm 51." As for his shortcomings in his family, Kip humbly shared,

*Though Elena and I believe that we raised our precious children in the Lord as each was baptized and remained faithful during their teen years, my biggest regret was that I put my children on a pedestal in front of the movement. This put too much pressure on them and hurt them spiritually as sometimes they felt that they could not measure-up. I have apologized to each of them for this. They have forgiven me, and we remain a very close family. I pray daily and believe with all of my heart that because of the godly training each received that one day, **"when they are [older],"** they will return to the Lord.*

God taught one last invaluable lesson to Kip about his sins in his leadership concerning the weak. He wrote,

*God has a sense of ironic justice. To rid Jacob of his deceitful nature, God placed Jacob under Laban, a worse deceiver. To show me how insensitive and in fact merciless at times I had been to the weak, God made me "weak" and placed me "under" upset and – from my point of view – unforgiving brothers who would not give me any mercy or the benefit of the doubt, though I felt I had done so much for them through the years. I felt humiliated through shame and exasperated to the point of considering leaving the Lord. I learned that mercy expressed through kindness, forgiveness and gentleness – was not only God's way to encourage and strengthen the weak, but the only path to keep a movement together. In all of these trials, my dear wife exemplified how one should love the weak by staying at my side with unconditional love.*

These lessons were painfully learned through the discipline of suffering that God allowed Kip *"as a son"* to endure. (Hebrews 12:5-11) However by July 2003, Kip – though severely weakened by these many trials – was a "changed man." He was refreshed by repentance, and so the Spirit sent him to Portland to build again with these lessons freshly etched on his heart. (Acts 3:19)

74

# THE DESTRUCTION OF A GLOBAL MOVEMENT

At the onset of the sabbatical – shocking to many of us – most of the World Sector Leaders failed to support the McKeans in their time of crisis. Some World Sector Leaders agreed that because of the unfaithfulness of McKeans' child, they were now unfit to lead. Some individuals were bitter and, in their words, "The McKeans have too high of expectations for us and our churches." While others, silent for years, now openly expressed, "Why do 'our churches' need to contribute money to HOPE*worldwide* and/or the Central Missions Fund?" So, the insidious desire to be autonomous as well as doubting whether the world could be evangelized in a generation began to permeate the World Sector Leaders, thus paralyzing them.

At this point, mercy, forgiveness and an ongoing support of the McKeans' leadership on the part of the World Sector Leaders would have saved the ICOC from its fall. Indeed, the McKeans humbly begged for the forgiveness of their sins and shortcomings on multiple occasions and even in tears shared Scriptures to this end. Yet, no mercy was extended as the World Sector Leaders cowered as there mounted a growing number of vociferous attacks on Kip and Elena. Clearly in retrospect at this juncture, a "domino effect" of "God's ironic justice" was again beginning to occur. As the World Sector Leaders had drawn back from the McKeans, so now most of the World Sector Leaders were being likewise undermined with no mercy by those under their leadership for the exact same issues: marriage dynamic, children's behavior, and leadership style.

This created a leadership vacuum. It was at this point that the Kingdom Teachers and Kingdom Elders chose to elevate themselves. (Of note, these two groups were composed entirely of people with their roots in the Mainline Church of Christ.) In fact, just three weeks after the McKeans were put on Sabbatical on September 1, 2001, Andy Fleming called a meeting of the Kingdom Teachers with the sole intent to take the ICOC back to Mainline theology, thus reuniting them with the Mainline Churches of Christ.

Andy and the other Kingdom Teachers were fueled by their feelings of under-appreciation and entitlement, as well as sentimentality toward their relatives still in the Mainline Churches of Christ. Very sadly, this bitter spirit and common denominational roots bonded the Kingdom Teachers and Kingdom Elders. Like Absalom, they initiated a very calculated campaign to *"steal the hearts of the men of Israel."* (2 Samuel 15:6) They heightened the issue of "unbelieving children disqualifying men from leadership" through a series of articles which appeared on the Los Angeles ICOC Website. Here, they also introduced their confusing "Mainline doctrines" of "consensus leadership" and "elders having authority over the very evangelists that appointed them."

In the Kingdom Elders' and Kingdom Teachers' lessons and local meetings, they viciously attacked the "hierarchical structure of the ICOC," in which they were subordinated to the McKeans and the World Sector Leaders. As stated before, this leadership pyramid was Kip's practical application of Exodus 18:13-26 and was the vehicle that the Spirit used to spread the Gospel to 171 nations. They cruelly assailed Kip further on his "forceful approach of leadership and preaching" labeling this: "Kip's militaristic style as a son of an admiral."

At the forefront of this ungodly rebellion were Andy Fleming, the leader of the Kingdom Teachers, and Scott Green, who were both World Sector Leaders with Mainline Church of Christ backgrounds. Fleming and Green, alongside Gordon Ferguson, Douglas Jacoby and Sam Laing – Kingdom Teachers – as well as Wyndham Shaw and Bruce Williams – Kingdom Elders – began a focused effort to "falsely" teach against the Biblical concept of a central

76

leadership with a central leader for God's people, thus returning the ICOC to the "Mainline theology" of autonomy. They used professed "wisdom" and proclaimed that these "better and more mature teachings" (James 3:13-16) – like autonomy and "discipling is optional not a command" – would make "the Kingdom" much "healthier." Sadly, but again clearly in retrospect, these "better teachings" and their "wisdom" only served to halt the expansion of God's Movement, confuse and scatter disciples, and save far fewer people.

In Matthew 7:15-16, Jesus preaches quite pointedly, ***"Watch out for false prophets. They come to you in sheep's clothing, but inwardly they are ferocious wolves. By their fruit you will recognize them."*** The Arabian wolf – a small, white wolf in Israel about whom Jesus referred – is very hard to distinguish from white sheep of similar size. They travel in packs ferociously devouring individual sheep and destroying whole flocks of sheep. Therefore, according to Jesus, the discerning Christian should examine very carefully the condition of the "spiritual flock" and be perceptive about who is a sheep and who is not.

Paul pointed out this same principle in 2 Corinthians 11:2-5 to the Corinthian Church in their drifting into false teachings that destroyed their fellowship:

> *I am jealous for you with a godly jealousy. I promised you to one husband, to Christ, so that I might present you to a pure virgin to Him. But I am afraid that just as Eve was deceived by the serpent's cunning, your minds may somehow be lead astray from your pure and sincere devotion to Christ. For is someone comes to you and preaches a Jesus other than the Jesus we already preached, or if you receive a different spirit from the one you already received, or a different Gospel from the one you accepted, you put up with it easily enough. I do not think I am in the least inferior to those "super-apostles."*

77

Very interestingly, the so-called *"super-apostles"* put down and undermined Paul's influence, suggesting that his teachings were *"inferior."* Paul – responding as a concerned father in the faith – challenged the church to see that they were "duped" (*"led astray"*) into following *"a different Jesus"* that affected the *"purity"* of their sold-out commitment to Christ. This same dynamic developed between the Kingdom Teachers and Kingdom Elders against Kip in 2001 - 2003 when they introduced Mainline theology into the Movement, thus *"preaching a different Jesus... with a different spirit."* Kip simply wanted the churches to have the same *"pure and sincere devotion to Christ"* that they had at baptism.

In 2 Corinthians 11:13-15, Paul revealed the true identity of these *"super-apostles"* – false teachers:

> *For such people are false apostles, deceitful workers, masquerading as Apostles of Christ. And no wonder, for Satan himself masquerades as an angel of light. It is not surprising, then, if his servants also masquerade as servants of righteousness. Their end will be what their actions deserve.*

Shockingly to most in Corinth, these men who were once esteemed Apostles had become "messengers of Satan." The same is true with the Kingdom Teachers and Kingdom Elders in regard to their teachings that led to the destruction of God's worldwide Movement – the ICOC. The problem now, as it was then, is that most ICOC disciples cannot conceive that men who influenced them for Christ through Kip's vision or world evangelism, now are in fact *"masquerading as servants of Christ"* and have become *"deceitful workers"* for Satan.

After the McKeans' sabbatical began in 2001, spearheading the "new direction" in the LA ICOC was Bruce Williams, my mentor for my first eight years as a disciple of Jesus. Williams opted to circulate the slander about the McKeans and the "new teachings" through "Family Talks," each consisting of about 20 Christians. Williams – heightened in his influence by the support of his fellow elder in the LA ICOC Al Baird, who had been a World Sector Leader and a father to Kip – travelled throughout the six-county area of metropolitan LA, falsely teaching the people that it was Kip's personality, his "militaristic style of leadership," and his inability to lead his own family that was the demise of our churches. Three deacons from Williams' own region and I openly challenged Williams, calling him to stop the slander.

Knowing that I had been in near daily contact with Baird as his personal computer consultant for two years, Williams contacted Baird and called me on a conference call. They insisted their "Family Talk" claims were well-known amongst the leadership and that they had the McKeans' full approval to talk about the situation with his kids. I immediately put into practice Proverbs 18:17 and attempted to "conference in" Kip. However, the moment Kip was added to the call both Williams and Baird disconnected and refused my calls to reconnect. In my ensuing conversation with Kip, I was heartbroken when I learned the real truth that the McKeans had never given such approval.

Later in 2003, Fleming, Williams and Baird – alongside former World Sector Leaders Marty Fuqua and Peter Garcia-Bengochea of LA – would perpetuate an unprecedented and unbiblical move. These men swayed those who held positions on the Board of Directors to use the authority given to them by the "laws of the United States" to supersede the "laws of the Scriptures." Fleming, Williams, Baird, Fuqua and Garcia-Bengochea used the Board of Directors to force out the leader whom they had wholeheartedly agreed for years was "God's man" – placed in authority by God to lead His Movement and maintain unity. I remember the shock and horror of learning in a 45-minute discussion with Andy Fleming that this was a thoroughly thought-out and executed plan. He preached to the Riverside Sector of the Los Angeles ICOC about our new *"freedom in Christ"* "boasting" to the congregation how "he" had Kip removed. After Fleming's lesson, he relayed to me more specifics.

Interestingly, there are many movements recorded in the Scriptures. Noah, Moses, Joshua, Nehemiah, David, John the Baptist and of course Jesus were all raised-up by God to lead remnants of God's people to become great movements. Near the end of their lives, both Gideon and David personally chose to step away from their positions. However, only one time in all of Scripture is the leader of one of God's movements ever "forced out" of his leadership position by the people he led. This occurred in Absalom's rebellion against David with Absalom suffering the consequence of death. (2 Samuel 15-18) In time, God raised-up David to lead again – just as He has now done with Kip. In the Bible, God always "raised-up" and "took out" His leader in "His" timing. God expected His people to trust Him and to wait on His timing instead of rebelling against Him and His leader.

Although the McKeans were "officially fired" in April 2003, this horrific and shameful event was never announced to any of the International Churches of Christ. Immediately following the firing of the McKeans, another series of articles about "unbelieving children" was circulated, which essentially began, "We have continued to study the topic of unbelieving children…" Here, these same teachers completely reversed their stance on "unbelieving children" – the very principle that was falsely used to "force out" God's leader. As of today, not one of the former World Sector Leaders, Kingdom Teachers or Kingdom Elders would say that an unfaithful child disqualifies an evangelist, because many of them have unfaithful children and presently serve as "Lead Evangelists." Sadly, this unspoken reversal of position – to now "protect" themselves – exposes the hypocritical evil of "using" the McKeans' child to "rid" the Movement of God's man.

The harsh and ungodly treatment of the McKeans in firing them from the ministry, as well as this "double standard" about "unfaithful children," would have led most couples to simply quit the "fish bowl life" of the ministry. Though severely wounded, what set the McKeans apart from most couples was their deep conviction that God had called them into the ministry, as well as their constant encouragement to each other to stay righteous before God and to continue to love their critics, not giving into Satan's temptations of hate, self-pity or "striking back."

Of special note, only one World Sector Leader – Pat Gempel – has publicly apologized to the McKeans. This she did in Portland at the 2005 World Missions Jubilee. It is also important to state that Kip has said, "I'll never condone in the New Movement anyone speaking out naming the men and women in leadership in the ICOC, whose children are unfaithful and especially which of their children have become unfaithful and left God. I have personally felt the devastation it causes in the lives of a family and especially in the lives of the children. I still love all of these families very much. Therefore, I would never intentionally hurt any of these children, as I pray that each of them will return to God and once more be a faithful disciple."

Sadly, the cruel public character assassination of both Kip and Elena using the spiritual condition of their children continues to this day. Yet, the sharp decline of members in the ICOC since the McKeans' sabbatical in 2001, testifies to God's hand being against this ungodly *"conspiracy."* (2 Samuel 15-18) In sharp contrast, the rapid increase of disciples and churches in God's new SoldOut Movement, which God has raised-up Kip to lead – alongside a loyal and unified team of overseeing evangelists, women's ministry leaders, and shepherding couples – testifies to God's approval! (1 Corinthians 3:7)

Another significant testimony of God pouring out His blessings when authentic discipling was restored is in marriage and family. For years, the ICOC *"boasted in the Lord"* to have very few divorces. With discipling

81

abandoned, divorce became rampant – even with couples who were at one time in the full-time ministry! In sharp contrast, in God's New Movement once again divorce is non-existent in most congregations, as the marriages and families are *"rejoicing in the Lord."*

The two most prominent aspects of Mainline theology (but hidden to many because of a lack of knowledge about the roots of the ICOC) were blindly adopted by most preachers in the ICOC: 1) Becoming only a "New Testament" Church – the Old Testament Scriptures (though historically accurate) had no authority, especially in the areas of leadership and governess. 2) The mode of the interpretation of Scripture by Thomas Campbell – "Speak where the Bible speaks, and be silent where the Bible is silent." Since the New Testament does not explicitly have the term World Sector Leaders, the Kingdom Elders and Kingdom Teachers swayed the rest of the leaders of the ICOC at the Long Beach Unity Meeting in November 2002, to completely dissolve the structured, central leadership. In shame, the McKeans and the World Sector Leaders who had not yet stepped down were "forced" to resign their roles at the Long Beach Unity Meeting. (However, the McKeans were still to be paid full-time and in January 2003 began serving in the Cal State Long Beach Campus Ministry.)

This upheaval embraced a reactionary "new and better vision" of congregations that were "so mature" that they no longer needed overseeing evangelists. Most also embraced consensus leadership in the local congregation with no "Lead Evangelist" – because the term "Lead Evangelist" is not found in the New Testament. At this time, a quest to eliminate a structured outreach (Bible Talks) and structured discipling (Discipleship Partners) arose. "Kip's vision" of the evangelization of the nations in a generation was called "a good idea" yet "impossible" by such outspoken critics as Douglas Jacoby and Scott Green. Some began to label Kip as a "false teacher" for this dream, believing that the pressure on the churches to evangelize the world in a generation was the primary source of bitterness in many leaders and in many churches. Yet devoid of the dream to change the world, Proverbs 29:18 would prove true again – *"Without vision the people perish."*

The ultimate demise of what was then known and revered as the International Church of Christ came in February 2003, when Henry Kriete, a hurting and former Mainline Church of Christ evangelist in London, released his letter entitled, *Honest To God.* In his letter, Kriete advocated "a time for anger and the overthrowing of temples: I believe the time is now." The rebellion of some of the World Sector Leaders and all of the Kingdom Elders and Kingdom Teachers was consequently passed on to all the members. Thousands left God confused and angry. Other disciples quietly "walked away" to try to find "the same church elsewhere," which proved to be in vain.

Further confusing the membership was the decision by the Kingdom Elders and Kingdom Teachers in April 2003 to "reopen the door to the Mainline Church of Christ." Kip – as a loving and concerned *"father in the faith"* – reminded and warned the LA leadership as well as what was left of the ICOC leadership that most members in the Mainline Church of Christ were not totally committed disciples. (1 Corinthians 4:14-17) He conveyed that trying to merge the "two fellowships" – ICOC and Mainline – would produce more confusion. Not heeding the words of "their prophet," as of today, the ICOC has lost its distinctiveness and identity. Very significantly, to signal a fundamental change of doctrine, almost all ICOC congregations no longer called themselves the "International Church of Christ," but paid legal fees to change their names back to simply the "Church of Christ." For example, the legal name of the Boston International Church of Christ became the Boston Church of Christ.

Satan's doctrine of autonomy had two more destructive effects on the ICOC: First of all, outside the United States autonomy gave birth to a "sinful nationalism." Many international congregations did not want their church led or overseen by "a foreigner." Consequently – just a month after the November 2002 Long Beach Unity Meeting – the London ICOC fired their Lead Evangelist, for the most part because he was American. After the 2003 Kriete Letter that called for an angry rebellion, scores of missionaries were rejected by "the nationals" they laid down their lives to convert. These same missionaries returned home in shame. Tragically, they then needed to find secular jobs, as the American congregations could not absorb the salaries of so many returning missionaries, especially with their own weekly contributions plummeting because of complete lack of confidence in leadership and a flagging conviction about the "need" for a worldwide movement.

Secondly, autonomy – and "the hypocritical desire for each preacher to lead his own kingdom" – very sadly led to the "one ICOC church in each city" dividing into several congregations of varying convictions. For example, London divided into six separate churches; Los Angeles splintered into seven congregations; and Atlanta separated into 12 congregations!

While the ICOC embraced these multiple congregations in one city as brothers, the SoldOut Movement is criticized for "planting new congregations" into cities such as these. The establishment of SoldOut Movement Churches in these cities does not condemn individuals who are saved as they continue to truly live as disciples in the ICOC's splintered congregations. The planting of these "new congregations" simply says we are going to evangelize the world, including cities which already have disciples who will not work in unity with us. Ironically in the 80's and 90's, the Mainline Churches of Christ made the same statement when the Boston Movement (ICOC) planted churches in "their" cities. The ICOC position then and ours now is: The need for "another church" is that we do not believe that any other congregation will evangelize that entire city, and thus the world. We believe we must obey this command of God, because though "our congregation" is not the only church with disciples, it is the only church composed of only disciples.

# FIRED BY MEN
# APPROVED BY GOD

In April 2003, the McKeans courageously confronted the LA ICOC leadership in the presence of Bob and Pat Gempel, who the McKeans asked to come as witnesses. Kip and Elena challenged Al Baird, Marty Fuqua, Andy Fleming, Bruce Williams and Peter Garcia-Bengochea on these issues: 1) Abandoning discipling; 2) Returning to Mainline theology – especially autonomy; 3) The silence – the deceit – about these decisions with the LA membership; 4) The silence – the deceit – to the LA membership about the incredible numbers leaving the ICOC around the world in every congregation – falling away or walking away; 5) Calling the dream of the evangelization of the nations in a generation, "Impossible." Kip and Elena reiterated at the meeting, "The dream of an evangelized world is not only possible, but it was accomplished in the first century and is the command of God." (Colossians 1:23; 1 Timothy 3:16, 4:9-11) At the conclusion of the meeting, the McKeans were fired for these convictions.

Now with little support from any disciples anywhere, Kip took his stand and wrote *Revolution Through Restoration – Part III: From Babylon To Zion*. In this treatise of faith, despite all the opposition and abandonment of many once faithful brothers, Kip realized all the more the sovereignty of God and how He used seemingly down and disastrous times as a means to propel the Gospel of Jesus around the globe. He also humbly assessed his leadership, as well as what was godly and right in the Boston Movement, which became the ICOC. He documented where his and others' sins and shortcomings were addressed with little or no mercy and forgiveness. Kip concluded that this lack of "agapé love" was ultimately responsible for the demise of what was once God's Movement.

# THE SPIRIT MOVES THE MCKEANS TO PORTLAND

Officially on July 11, 2003, at the invitation of the leadership of the Portland International Church of Christ, Kip and Elena moved to Portland, Oregon to lead a hurting and devastated church. When the Kriete Letter came out in February 2003, the Portland Church had 300 members. Yet at the McKeans' first midweek just five months later in July 2003, it was only necessary to set up 25 chairs for the entire congregation! Over the next three years, the Portland Church experienced incredible growth to 487 members with over 600 in attendance on Sundays. Astonishingly, during the years following the Kriete Letter, the Portland International Church of Christ – under Kip's seasoned leadership – was the fastest growing congregation of what was left of the International Churches Of Christ in the world!

The Spirit's revival of the Portland Church centered in Kip's faith in preaching the Word and his uncompromising but "now gentle call" for every member's heart to obey it. Bible Talks, Discipleship Partners, a College/Teen Devotional, and the weekly contribution collections were quickly reinstated. The turning point came early on when Kip, though weakened but faithful and wiser after two years of intense suffering, called for an "Evening of Atonement." On Wednesday evening, August 13, 2003, over 100 people gathered to share their repentance to God and to each other publicly. Tony Untalan and Jeremy Ciaramella were the first to share, apologizing with tears and mentioning specific people in the crowd that they had sinned against. It moved everyone to tears. The heartfelt apologies and sharing by about 25 more individuals lasted almost three hours! In the following weeks, the Portland Church witnessed several baptisms and all realized that God was blessing their repentance. As well, during the Fall about 75 members returned to the church, who had left after the Kriete Letter. By January 2004, the Portland Church numbered about 120

87

disciples and word began to spread across America and in fact around the globe that "things were happening in Portland!" Over the next three years, individuals from 26 of the 50 states in the USA moved to Portland where many exclaimed upon their arrival as my wife and I did, "This is the church I was baptized in!" It was such a powerful time that a young couple – who moved from Ohio to be a part of the growing revival in the perpetually rainy city of Portland – wrote about their experience in a song:

## THE PORTLAND SONG

*Wasting – away here*
*When it was suddenly revealed*
*That we couldn't make it here without rain!*
*What a shame!*
*Patiently waiting, begging God constantly praying*
*Please lead us to greener pastures!*

*God is there anywhere to go?*
*Is there any hope to grow again?*
*Where are the people that still dream?*
*Please bring us times of refreshin'.*
*Then He sent hope from the West Coast!*
*There's plenty of rain on the West Coast!*

*Welcome to Portland, Oregon*
*Where the rain is pourin'*
*Hope your soul feels at home.*
*All the people criticizin'*
*But we are just baptizin'*
*Got plenty of H20!*
*And you say hey-o welcome home!*
*And you say hey-o welcome home!*

*Came here with nothing*
*But with the faith*
*God could do something great!*
*Now this was more than we asked for*

*That's for sure!*
*You shared your faith*
*You shared your dreams*
*Gave us love*
*Helped us to believe*
*You were the answer to our prayer!*
*God provided a place to go*
*He gave us hope to grow again!*
*And here are the people that still dream*
*Now are the times of refreshin'.*
*And we found hope on the West Coast!*
*There's plenty of rain on the West Coast!*

*Welcome to Portland, Oregon*
*Where the rain is pourin'*
*Hope your soul feels at home.*
*All the people criticizin'*
*But we are just baptizin'*
*Got plenty of H2O!*
*And you say hey-o welcome home!*
*And you say hey-o welcome home!*

Listen on YouTube: https://youtu.be/NPiV1n3YDB4!

# THE GLOBAL INTERNET MINISTRY BEGINS

In the early days of Portland to propel the message that God put on his heart, Kip relied heavily on Jeremy Ciaramella to build a website that would appeal to the faithful remnant around the world. The name Upsidedown21 (USD21) was selected; *"Upsidedown"* since the first century church *"turned the world upsidedown"* (Acts 17:6 RSV), and the **"21"** gave the vision that the disciples' impact in the first century would be echoed in the twenty-first century! The weekly bulletin articles of the Portland Church were displayed on the USD21 Website. Quite creatively, these articles were translated into seven other languages also displayed on the website. Feedback from the website was tremendous! Most of the people that ended up moving to Portland first became interested through the articles and Kip's sermons online. Kip realized there was an entirely new frontier for unifying the people of God and evangelizing the world in a generation. This led him to yet another innovation, the appointing of Jeremy Ciaramella as the first CyberEvangelist at the 2004 Jubilee!

ICC Hot News covered church plantings
all around the world!

Also, in 2004, Kip published in the *Portland Bulletin* positive feedback which he had received in emails about the bulletin articles, which he called, "Good News Emails." In 2008, the *Good News Email* became a monthly report by Kip of all God was doing in the SoldOut Movement. The *Good News Email* not only strengthened the unity of the Movement, but also was a vehicle to bring several remnant disciples into the Movement. In 2009, I was greatly humbled when Kip asked me to serve as the Lead CyberEvangelist for the SoldOut Movement's Global Internet Ministries. Of tremendous encouragement to me are my fellow CyberEvangelists: Jeremy Ciaramella, Rob Onekea, Jake Studer, Joshua Ajayi, Elliot Svenkenson, Lance Underhill, Chuck Hess, AJ Penedo, Albert Wagers, Jose Otero, Alex Rhode – as well as our CyberWomen's Ministry Leaders: Jacque Econonio, Melanie Coyle and Chantelle Anderson!

The SoldOut Movement CyberEvangelists!

# THE PORTLAND CONTROVERSY

In June 2004, just eleven months after coming to Portland, Kip and the Portland Church hosted the first World Missions Jubilee entitled, THE LORD OF THE FELLOWSHIP. Many leaders of the ICOC attended – some genuinely interested in the incredible growth in the Portland Church; others came skeptical, even scornful. Trying desperately to bring reform, repentance and unity to what remained of the ICOC, Kip asked several of the more influential leaders in what remained of the ICOC to speak on the program. Most accepted this invitation. However, controversy soon followed as Kip delivered one of the most impassioned pleas for world evangelism through *"making disciples"* in his message, A Great Light Has Dawned.

In the summer of 2005, the World Missions Jubilee was entitled UPSIDEDOWN21. It was on this momentous occasion after prayer and fasting that Kip decided that the only way to salvage the ICOC as a discipling movement was by "calling out the remnant." Even greater controversy followed. In September, in reaction to Kip's "calling out the remnant," he was "uninvited" by Scott Green from speaking at the ICOC Leadership Meeting in Seattle set for early September 2005.

Adding fuel to the Spirit's fire, Chris and Sonja Chloupek – former high-profile ministry leaders in the LA ICOC who had moved to Phoenix – visited the Portland Church in late September 2005. After experiencing a personal revival that weekend, the Chloupeks felt compelled to confront Gordon Ferguson, a former Kingdom Teacher and the then preacher for the "very Mainline" Phoenix Valley Church of Christ – formerly the Phoenix International Church of Christ. They challenged him from the Scriptures on the lukewarmness in the Phoenix Church, as well as about the hundreds of disciples that had fallen or walked away. They appealed to

Ferguson to ask Kip for help. In anger, Ferguson refused to seek help. Seeing his hardness of heart, the Chloupeks asked Kip if he would back them in starting what came to be known as the first "remnant group." Now, all around the world, the term "Portland Movement" began to be whispered with the hope of a new day!

In Phoenix, Chris and Sonja Chloupek courageously initiated the very first SoldOut Movement Remnant Group in their home in 2005!

Contrary to democratic "Western thinking" where the "majority is always right," on many occasions in the Scriptures, the "minority report" is the one that is of God. (Numbers 13:26-33; Matthew 7:13-14) Even in Elijah's day, the question was surely asked, "Can 450 prophets of Baal be wrong, and one prophet of God be right?" Sensing people were *"wavering between two opinions,"* in October 2005, 65 evangelists and elders from what remained of the International Churches of Christ wrote a letter criticizing Kip as a *"troubler of Israel."* (1 Kings 18:17-21) Not realizing that Jesus *"came to bring... division"* (Luke 12:51) and not comprehending that divisiveness is of God when someone preaches the Word like Jesus, they confronted Kip on being "divisive." (John 10:19)

There were four false charges against Kip: 1) His words were "unwholesome" and thus divisive, as he called the ICOC Churches "lukewarm." Though Kip indeed called the ICOC lukewarm, but like Jesus in Revelation 3:19, Kip courageously challenged them because of his love for them. 2) The charge of divisiveness was also leveled against Kip as scores of move-ins to Portland were called "sheep stealing" instead of the Spirit moving them to a place of revival. (Jeremiah 23:3-4) 3) Kip was again called divisive because he accepted the invitation of evangelists in other places – such as Raul Moreno in Santiago, Chile – to disciple their lives and churches. Yet Kip was graciously responding to their plea for help and fellowship. In Raul's own words, "We were completely abandoned when overseeing evangelists were eliminated and called 'unbiblical.'" 4) Kip supported any group of disciples that gathered from what was left of the ICOC to start a new church of "sold-out disciples." Interestingly, some remnant groups formed seeking revival even before many heard of the Portland/SoldOut Movement.

A forceful yet humble response letter entitled, *A Concern For All The Churches* was written by Kip and the leaders of the Portland International Church of Christ. A second letter was written in response to Portland's *A Concern For All The Churches.* This second letter, once again was subtly asking people, "Can all of us be wrong?" was signed by 85 leaders in what was left of the ICOC now hopelessly plagued with Mainline theology. This sinful letter officially marked Kip and those who followed his gallant leadership as "divisive" and not to be associated with. Jesus warned, ***"All this I have told you so that you will not go astray. They will put you out of the synagogue [disfellowshipment]; in fact, a time is coming when anyone who kills you will think he is offering a service to God. They will do such things because they have not known the Father or me."*** (John 16:1-3)

However, as time has passed, many disciples around the world like me understood that envy, jealousy and insecurity were at the root of these attacks. (Psalm 106:16) Of grave concern, cynics labeled these events as simply "church politics" instead of what it truly was: An epic confrontation for the hearts of the remnant and the lost souls of the world. Inspired by Kip's stand that Autumn and his nine-part series in the *Portland Bulletin: God's Mandate For World Evangelism,* the Kiev (Ukraine) Remnant Group of 25 disciples was formed in December 2005. This was the first of many remnant groups established by the Spirit outside the United States!

# THE BIRTH OF THE SOLDOUT MOVEMENT

Despite all of the criticisms from within the ICOC, the Portland Church continued to multiply disciples through not only baptisms, but through more and more "remnant disciples" moving to Portland to find spiritual revival and refreshment. Also after much prayer, Chris and Theresa Broom – leaders of the Central New York Church of Christ – made a bold decision in early 2006 to call their entire congregation to "fully join" with Kip. In June 2006, the Brooms led a mission team composed of Syracuse and Portland disciples to plant the Chicago International Christian Church. The mission team joined a small remnant group already in Chicago. In many ways, this was the first "church planting" of what was clearly becoming a new movement!

In time, the Central New York Church of Christ was renamed the Syracuse International Christian Church. From this small but heartsy congregation of 120 sold-out Christians came such future leaders as Andrew and Patrique Smellie, Chris and Kerri-Sue Adams, as well as Roger and Kama Parlour and their children – Joel and Brittany. For its incredible sacrifice of disciples and finances for God and His New Movement, the Syracuse Church became known as "the little church that could... and did." Sadly, the Brooms became deceitful and for years hid that they had forsaken their earlier stated convictions about central leadership, discipling and world evangelism. Theresa was disfellowshipped for contempt in 2016. Chris followed her and left the Movement in mid-2017.

In July 2006, the Spirit sent a 14-member mission team from Portland to Phoenix dauntlessly led by Matt and Helen Sullivan. Having been inspired by the 2004 Jubilee, the Sullivans were "remnant disciples" who moved from the decimated Fresno, California ICOC to Portland to find revival and to train for the ministry. Combining the mission team and the remnant group in Phoenix, the Sullivans built a rock-solid *"foundation."* (1 Corinthians 3:10-11) Through discipling, they raised-up Chris and Sonja Chloupek as well as Luke and Brandyn Speckman into the full-time ministry. In 2008, the Spirit sent the Sullivans and a small mission team to join the remnant group in Santiago, Chile. Thus, the Santiago International Christian Church became the first international planting of the SoldOut Movement! In turn, the Phoenix Church was dynamically led by the Chloupeks and the campus ministry was served by the Speckmans.

In Santiago, the Sullivans repeated their building of a solid *"foundation"* of disciples as they did in Phoenix. In turn, Raul and Lynda Moreno – the valiant leaders of Santiago – moved to Los Angeles for healing and training. Lynda has expressed on many occasions that she suffered a "nervous breakdown" at the collapse of what was once God's Movement – the ICOC – and the desertion of her "friends" in the ICOC. This only intensified when the Morenos joined God's New Movement thus starting the Santiago Remnant Group.

In 2010, the Chloupeks moved to Los Angeles for more training and to initiate a new AMS (Arts Media Sports) Ministry. Very revealing is that the autonomous AMS Region of the old LA ICOC changed its name and incorporated under the name "Turning Point Church." Its leaders received certification and much of their ministry direction from the Saddleback Community Church – a denominational church that does not believe in baptism *"for the remission of sins."* (Acts 2:38) In fact, posted on the Los Angeles ICOC Website were job openings for Intern, Sector Leader and Region Leader which carried a prerequisite of completing the Saddleback Church's "Purpose-Driven Church Training Program."

This dangerous doctrinal drift – with the pleasing appeal of "open-mindedness" – is also seen on the International

Teaching Ministry Website of Douglas Jacoby. Jacoby has become the most prominent of the former "Kingdom Teachers" as Fleming's writings are regarded as of "little weight," as his Birmingham, England Church averaged only seven baptisms a year – which is less than the Mainline Church of Christ. On Jacoby's website, which contains some very good commentaries on the Scriptures making it credible, he posts such articles as *Baptism Revisited* by John Lang. Lang teaches that the Baptist Church position on salvation before baptism is valid: "There is no conclusive Biblical support for the view that God rejects baptized, repentant believers simply because they believed that their salvation coincided with their point of faith rather than their baptism… [Therefore], we should be honest about our limitations and acknowledge our inability to precisely determine 'who is and who is not a Christian'." This is a "Satanic false teaching" from a false teacher *"masquerading as a servant of righteousness."* (2 Corinthians 11:13-15) Yet Jacoby writes in his introduction of this article, "I appreciate brothers like John…"

Most in the ICOC in the 90's "believed" that their leaders were completely unified, but this was never the case. During Kip's years of leadership in the ICOC, his biggest challenge was unity. He was constantly encouraging, striving and "battling" with those in leadership to bring everyone to unity on the aforementioned Bible convictions "to replace" their traditional beliefs from their Mainline roots. Ultimately, this disunity of doctrine was a key reason that led to the fracturing of the once genuinely close relationships among the leaders. This disconnect between disciples now extends throughout the entire ICOC.

In August 2006, the Third World Missions Jubilee was celebrated! It was aptly entitled, **FOLLOW THE FIRE**. In attendance was the new full-time minister from the Hilo International Church of Christ, Kyle Bartholomew. Kyle was converted in 2001 from the University of Hawaii – Hilo. He was the star and the captain of their basketball team. With

Kyle's influence, eventually all five starters of the UH Hilo Basketball Team were disciples! Confident and charismatic, Kyle humbly realized that he was untrained for the work of the ministry. After participating in the Jubilee, he asked Kip and Elena to disciple him and his wife, Joan. Upon being asked to disciple Kyle, Kip asked Kyle, "Do you realize how controversial the Portland Church is? If I disciple you, you will become equally as controversial." Without any hesitation, Kyle responded, "I see no other possible alternative for my wife and me, and no hope for Hilo if you do not come." Interestingly, Kyle was fully supported in this decision by his two younger brothers – Evan and Levi – and by most in the Hilo Leadership Group. However, less than half of the membership was behind this radical resolution.

In the *May 25, 2008 City of Angels International Christian Church Bulletin,* Kyle wrote an article entitled, *Hope For The Islands!* He recapped the history of discipling ministries in the Hawaiian Islands including his conversion:

*When I was baptized as a disciple on July 29, 2001 through the efforts of the Hilo International Church of Christ, I was blown away by the commitment, passion and love that I saw in each and every disciple. What inspired me most was the dream that each disciple shared to evangelize the Islands, the Pacific Rim and ultimately the world in their generation. In 2001, there were about 60 disciples in Hilo, 75 in Maui and around 1,000 in Oahu – every disciple believed this dream was possible, and so did I!*

*Sadly, in November 2002 after the ICOC leadership's decision to return to a more Mainline Church of Christ theology, as well as the advent of the "Kriete Letter" in early 2003, so many beloved aspects of 'my church' began to change. Gone was a fellowship where every member was a practicing disciple of Jesus. Gone was the deep love for one another through discipling relationships. And gone was the dream to evangelize the*

*Islands and the world. By 2006, membership was declining at an alarming rate! Oahu dropped from 1,000 disciples to 200; Hilo went from almost 60 disciples to 38; and Maui was reduced from 75 disciples to 25. Oahu went from six full-time couples to two, and both Hilo and Maui went from a full-time couple leading each congregation to untrained volunteers, as vision and then contribution plummeted. Baptisms became extremely rare, restorations were almost non-existent, and there had not been a single church planted from the Islands for over six long years. It was obvious to me that something needed to change!*

*In late 2006, I was asked by the "leadership group" of the Hilo ICOC to be the full-time minister. They were indeed desperate as the Hilo Church had not had a baptism for almost two years! Since I was untrained, I was convinced we needed additional help. Therefore, in considering which church to ask for help, I decided to attend the Portland World Missions Jubilee. I was so in awe of God so obviously working through the Portland Church, as the fastest growing church in the ICOC at that time, that I asked Kip and Elena to disciple Joan and me. Thankfully, they agreed. One month later, the McKeans came to help us rebuild the Hilo Church's foundation to be composed of only disciples. (1 Corinthians 3:10-11) After an eventful weekend of Kip's and Elena's preaching, God left us with a "Gideon-like" twelve disciples, whose dream was to once again evangelize the world in our generation! The other 26 members, many of whom were lukewarm, started a new congregation with the help of evangelists from both the LA ICOC and the Oahu Church of Christ. Not having a baptism for almost two years in Hilo, yet starting with twelve sold-out disciples, God blessed us with 20 baptisms that next year! Sadly, yet to the point, the congregation that was started in opposition to Kip's and my vision of world evangelism through*

100

*God's plan of discipling still has not seen a baptism to this day.*

*Upon the McKeans' return to Portland, the Portland leaders, as well as others who believed in Jesus' dream for the evangelization of the nations in one generation, pleaded with Kip to realize that God was initiating a "New Movement" by calling him to start again. On October 15, 2006, compelled by the Spirit, Kip published in the Portland Church Bulletin the first of a three-part series entitled,* **Partners In The Gospel**. *Though the names "Portland Movement" and "SoldOut Movement" had been used by detractors for over a year, these three articles were the formal announcement of the birth of a new family of churches – a new Movement of God!*

I personally was so encouraged by the events of August, September and October 2006. At the request of my dear wife who listened to sermons on the *Upsidedown21 Website* and read every bulletin, I visited the Portland Church in late August, one week before the Jubilee. After just one service, I went up to Kip and said, "This is the church I was baptized in! I'm moving my family here as soon as possible." I then came the following week to the FOLLOW THE FIRE JUBILEE and after confessing my sins associated with my lukewarmness, I moved my family to Portland on September 1, 2006. Shortly afterwards, Tracy at communion shared, "I finally have 'my Ron' back!" What Tracy meant was that when the ICOC made "discipling optional" (in reality for me non-existent), I had gone back to being my "old self" – a stranger to Tracy since we met and married in the church. However, through discipling, my *"first love"* for God was restored and I began to *"do the things [that I] did at first."* (Revelation 2:4-5) In other words, I was a sold-out disciple again, and thus once more "the Ron" with whom Tracy had fallen in love!

# THE SPIRIT TAKES THE MCKEANS TO LOS ANGELES

Inspired by divine wisdom, Jesus launched and centered the First Century Movement of disciples not in the small towns of Galilee where He for the most part ministered, but in the largest of Jewish cities – Jerusalem. An interesting similarity to Jesus' three years in Galilee before going to Jerusalem are the McKeans' three years in Portland. Realizing that the size and accessibility of the city of Portland was limiting for a worldwide movement, the McKeans laid a fleece before God about where to move. The Lord put upon their heart to move to either New York City or Los Angeles. The fleece was simple: Wherever a remnant group came out first, this would be the place from which to build again. In late October 2006, God answered the prayer with a small remnant group forming in Los Angeles – gathered by the Spirit working through Sal and Patricia Velasco and my wife and me. Though composed of only 23 disciples, the persecution was quite vicious and spearheaded by John Causey, who also had sent evangelists and elders to Hilo to oppose Kip and Kyle just a month before.

Kip and I both felt that it would be best if I moved back to LA to stabilize the remnant group. Just before my return, a formal letter was sent out by the LA ICOC Leadership wrongly "disfellowshipping" Kip, Sal Velasco, myself and "the splinter group" which is now the City of Angels International Christian Church. (John 16:1-3, 12:42-44) Without question, the LA ICOC Leadership – overseeing a congregation of less than 5,000 – felt threatened as they had witnessed over 5,000 of their members walk away or fall away since the Kriete Letter and the unjust firing of the McKeans. The following is an excerpt from the October 17, 2006 letter from the LA ICOC Leadership to all of its members:

102

*We are publicly marking Kip McKean, the force behind these efforts, Sal Velasco, the local leader of this faction, and whoever else promotes this action with them. We are all <u>commanded</u> by God's Word to "to keep away from them" (Romans 16:17) and "have nothing to do with them." (Titus 3:10) To communicate clearly, this means:*

1. *Do not attend any of their meetings.*
2. *Do not engage in any conversations with them about their group or the LA Church.*
3. *Do not allow anyone to deceive you or cause you to rationalize or minimize the sinfulness of these actions.*
4. *This applies not only to your contact with Kip McKean, Sal Velasco and Ron Harding, but also with <u>anyone</u> associated with this splinter group.*
5. *It is important to understand that anyone who joins this faction will no longer be considered in fellowship with the LA Church.*

Many have unknowingly perpetuated the false statement that only Kip was disfellowshipped, as they simply could not believe that a congregation of almost 1,000 zealous disciples which was baptizing scores of people would be disfellowshipped. Yet, the fifth point in the LA ICOC letter of October 17, 2006 clearly states that all in God's New Movement were disfellowshipped.

In late 2006, Kip and Elena – seeing the hand of God leading them – came to Los Angeles to minister to the remnant group and to climb their beloved "Mt. Shalom" (aka Mt. Hollywood) to vow to God that they would be faithful to His vision to the end. By January 2007, plans had been made to raise $150,000 to send a 42-disciple mission team from Portland to Los Angeles. The leadership of the Portland Church was given to Steve and Lisa Johnson.

The Inaugural Service of the City of Angels International Christian Church was May 6, 2007, and in fact, was the "official beginning" of the SoldOut Movement. We had an amazing attendance of 324! The 2007 World Missions Jubilee was held in Portland that summer, because Kip felt that the young church planting in LA should not be distracted with all of the necessary preparations for a Jubilee. Also, to encourage the Portland Church, the McKeans wanted to return with many of the newly baptized disciples from the mission team's efforts. This would demonstrate that the Portland Church's sacrifice of disciples and finances was more than worth it. The theme of the Jubilee was KING OF KINGS!

Kip very prayerfully and with trustworthy counselors chose the name "International Christian Church" for the New Movement's congregations for three reasons: 1) The name "International" conveyed the world vision of the New Movement. 2) "International" would also signal to the remnant that we are a revival movement out of the shattered "International" Church of Christ. 3) "Christian" because Kip's view of Scripture from a Restoration Movement historical perspective was closer to the conservative Christian Church's position: "Anything is permissible as long as it does not contradict the Bible," verses the Church of Christ: "Speak where the Bible speaks..." which means that one needs a command, example or necessary inference to name or have a particular practice.

By the end of the first year of the City of Angels Church in May 2008, 104 had been baptized into Christ – one more baptism than Kip and Elena's first year in Boston! Kip's rare ability to raise-up effective evangelists was once again witnessed as early on in the second year and unparalleled in the history of discipling churches in America, the Spirit sent-out the City of Angels Church's first two mission teams: Honolulu and New York City. In August 2008, the fourth World Missions Jubilee was held in Los Angeles and entitled, DECLARE HIS GLORY AMONG THE NATIONS. At this momentous event, not only was the New York City Mission Team officially sent out, but the Washington DC Mission Team, led by Andrew and Patrique Smellie and

104

composed of disciples from Syracuse and Eugene (Portland's planting in 2004), was sent out as well! Yet the highlight of the Jubilee was Kip's announcement of the forming of the Central Leadership Council (CLC) of the SoldOut Movement! Present World Sector Leaders that were in the "transitory" Central Leadership Council were: Nick and Denise Bordieri, Tim and Lianne Kernan, Andrew and Patrique Smellie, Matt and Helen Sullivan, Tony and Therese Untalan, and of course, the McKeans.

Later, my dear brother and sister Michael and Sharon Kirchner were added to the CLC for Michael to become the Administrator of the SoldOut Movement. Previous to moving to LA, Michael served as a Vice President of General Mills in Minneapolis, Minnesota. He gave-up this "dream job" – literally sacrificing millions of dollars in future earnings – to join God's New Movement in Los Angeles in the summer of 2007, as he like Moses *"regarded disgrace for the sake of Christ as of greater value than the treasures of [the American dream], because he was looking ahead to his reward."* (Hebrews 11:26)

Michael and Sharon Kirchner are the Administration Couple for the SoldOut Movement Churches.

Another historic decision announced at the 2008 Jubilee was the creation of MERCY*worldwide*. In the Boston

Movement, the benevolent arm of the church was called HOPE*worldwide*. "HOPE" was officially founded in 1991 under the leadership of Bob and Pat Gempel, with the World Sector Leaders as the Board of Directors and Kip as the Chairman of the Board. HOPE became one of the most powerful and respected religious charities in the world as all the members of every church could be mobilized as volunteers, thus having a "worldwide" impact. Eventually, HOPE had projects in almost 100 countries. HOPE's impact declined rapidly when the ICOC churches became autonomous. No longer could disciples be mobilized for worldwide projects, but also many church leaders had no desire to continue to fund a "centralized" organization. Interestingly, HOPE was officially founded in 1991 in the twelfth year of the Boston Movement. MERCY was founded in only the second year of the SoldOut Movement!

By 1995, the global impact of HOPE*worldwide* was so great that Kip as Chairman of the Board of HOPE was able to present to Nelson Mandela the "HOPE Unity Award" at the "South African White House" in Pretoria. Kip now serves as Chairmen of the Board for MERCY*worldwide*.

Nick and Denise Bordieri are dear friends of the
McKeans from the first days of Portland!

Kip never forgot how HOPE had opened the door of
evangelism to many nations, such as India and Israel.
Therefore, creating a "new HOPE" was a very high priority
in his desire to fulfill Jesus' dream of the evangelization of
the nations in this generation. Kip appointed as the Directors
of "MERCY" – Nick and Denise Bordieri, one of the most
heartsy couples that Kip and Elena had ever known.

As Chairman of the Board of MERCY, Kip looks
forward to the many opportunities to
serve the poor and needy!

107

# THE PORTLAND CHURCH
# IS LED ASTRAY

Also, at the 2008 Jubilee, the travesty of Steve and Lisa Johnson's abandonment (a second time) from Kip and Elena and Jesus' dream for the evangelization of the nations in a generation became apparent. I will never forget in his Jubilee speech, Steve foreshadowing their eminent departure from the Movement with the ominous opening words, "This is probably the last time I will be speaking to you at the Jubilee." I was caught completely off guard because previous to the Jubilee, Steve and I had almost weekly Skype times where we mutually encouraged one another. We discussed some very challenging topics, but I had no idea what he was really planning.

Two weeks after the Jubilee, Steve Johnson officially broke away from the SoldOut Movement, when he delivered a Wednesday Midweek sermon on autonomy. The week before this sermon, I had several conversations with Steve where he finally disclosed to me his true beliefs on discipling, autonomy and authority. He then told me that he was going to separate. This hurtful decision was precipitated by not wanting to pay a price that he and Lisa deemed too high to remain in the New Movement – the losing of most of their relationships in the ICOC because of the disfellowshipment of the entire New Movement and the passive distain inside Mainline Churches – their roots. Though subtly taught by the Johnsons after the Spirit had sent the McKeans to LA, now the Johnsons came out and vehemently opposed a central leadership with a central leader for a family of churches.

Largely through the efforts of Jeremy Ciaramella – the minister for the Eugene Church – a Portland Remnant Group quickly formed in reaction to the Johnsons' betrayal and unbiblical teachings. These heroic souls could not conceive of participating in a very staid Mainline worship service, into which the Portland Church immediately morphed. Upon news of this incident, critics seized the opportunity to attack Kip, Elena and God's young Movement. The Johnsons' deceit-filled departure from the SoldOut Movement directly caused the Portland Church to crash from 600 to less than 200 in attendance.

Kip and Elena selected Ron and Tracy Harding to be the new Portland International Christian Church Leaders in late 2008!

The formation of the Portland Remnant Group was essential in Kip's mind to reestablish a dynamic discipling ministry in Portland, since the city was the origin of the SoldOut Movement. After prayer and fasting, my wife and I graciously accepted the invitation to lead a mission team from LA to Portland. I told Kip that I needed time to speak with Steve before we made any announcements so that I could honor Steve's and my relationship. I called Steve and told him that I was not coming to Portland to be against him, but because he was refusing to work with us. I also conveyed that I still had the hope of having fellowship with one another. Since I was a professional drag racer for five years before I became a Christian, we agreed to go to the races at Portland International Raceway when I arrived. Sadly, Steve never returned another call of mine after my arrival in Portland. The Portland Remnant Group joined the mission team in late 2008. In Portland, God has vindicated Kip's call for a new Movement where every member in every church is "sold-out." After the sending of the mission team, the vibrant and new "Portland International Christian Church" quickly grew larger than the now stagnated "Portland Church of Christ" which used to be called the Portland International Church of Christ. This congregation remains autonomous to this day. As well, they have changed their name to simply the Portland Church of Christ, re-aligning themselves with Mainline Church of Christ doctrine.

Very important to everyone wanting to *see for themselves* what happened was the release one of the *April 5, 2009 City of Angels Church Bulletin* entitled, *History Speaks for Itself!* The article enables God's people the ability to be "Bereans" and study for themselves the history of their faith from 1979 till the present by providing PDF articles of every article written from the days of Boston till present. To this day, this collection of articles allows every individual disciple to read with their own eyes what all of their leaders put in writing and gives everyone the ability to test the words of all involved and so be *Empowered* to "test the spirits" (1 John 4:1-6) and clearly *see the truth* of where God's favor resides!

CITY OF ANGELS
INTERNATIONAL CHRISTIAN CHURCH

HOLLYWOOD

APRIL 5, 2009                                         VOLUME 3 • ISSUE 11

# History Speaks For Itself!
## Releasing The McKean Ministry Bulletins: 1979 – Present
### Cyber-Evangelist: Ron Harding

*"What has been will be again, what has been done will be done again; there is nothing new under the sun. Is there anything of which one can say, "Look! This is something new?" It was here already, long ago; it was here before our time." Ecclesiastes 1:9-10*

History is "His story!" Both sacred and secular history is the record of God's interactions with mankind. Yet, as Solomon wrote in Ecclesiastes, *"What has been will be again, what has been done will be done again."* As many historians have noted, "History repeats itself." The men of Issachar joined David's small, "divisive," but rapidly growing movement, because they *"understood the times and knew what Israel should do."* (1 Chronicles 12:32) The best approach to understanding our times and what "spiritual Israel" – disciples – should do, is to parallel our recent history with the corresponding Biblical times. Thus, "history speaks for itself." For this reason, we are releasing – on the SoldOut Movement websites – all of the bulletins during the epic years of Kip McKean's Ministry beginning in Lexington, a suburb of Boston (1979-1989) to Los Angeles (1990-2001) through his sabbatical (2001-2003) to Portland (2003-2007) and back to Los Angeles, where he serves the City of Angels International Christian Church (2007- present). Particularly exciting in the bulletins are the detailed documentations of all the Boston Movement and SoldOut Movement church plantings – highlighted by the church plantings Kip and Elena personally led: Manila, Philippines (1989); Bangkok, Thailand (1989); Moscow, Russia (1991); St. Petersburg, Russia (1992); and Los Angeles (2007), as well as their life-threatening days of leading the church in Cairo, Egypt (1989).

*Kip McKean*

Sacred history has provided movement after movement from which to search for parallels to our times. There are the "movements" of Adam; Noah; Moses; each of the judges; David; the kingships of Judah – especially Asa, Hezekiah and Josiah; the return of the Babylonian exiles to Zion; and Jesus' Movement – the first century church – which evangelized the world in their generation. (Colossians 1:23) Thought provoking parallels to our day can also be found in secular history by researching such movements as Luther's Protestant Reformation; Loyola's Jesuit Counter-Reformation Movement; the Methodist Movement of the Wesley brothers; Alexander Campbell's Christian Connection (Restoration) Movement and its divisions – the Disciples of Christ, the Mainline Church of Christ, the Conservative Christian Churches; the Crossroads (Campus Ministry) Total Commitment Movement; the Boston Movement – the International Churches of Christ; and presently, the new SoldOut Discipling Movement. Most of these movements, recorded in both sacred and secular history, start from a very small remnant with one leader, which God builds into a great nation – sadly, only to crumble by apostasy. Then, God starts again with a new remnant.

Every article from God's Modern-Day Movement
can still be found at http://history.usd21.org

111

# THE CROWN OF THORNS PROJECT

The theme for the 2009 Global Leadership Conference (GLC) was GO INTO ALL THE WORLD. It was held in early August and leaders from 20 different nations travelled to Los Angeles to participate. The following is a section of Kip's account of this amazing GLC as recorded in the *City of Angels Church Bulletin of August 16, 2009:*

> At the end of the lesson, I presented The Crown of Thorns Project. Remember that Jesus said to the faithful Eleven, **"You will be my witnesses in Jerusalem, and in all Judea and Samaria, and to the ends of the earth."**
>
> The Spirit has made Los Angeles the **"Jerusalem"** of God's New Movement. So, to evangelize the world, we must evangelize our **"Judea and Samaria"** – the United States and Canada. In just three years of existence, the SoldOut Movement has planted dynamic discipling churches in the four most influential cities of America – New York City, Los Angeles, Chicago and Washington DC – as well as in Portland, Honolulu, Hilo, Syracuse, Eugene and Phoenix. These churches do not include several heroic remnant churches. The US congregations [alongside our future first world congregations such as London and Paris] will provide the needed resources – disciples and finances – to go **"to the ends of the earth."** Therefore... we must plan to encircle the globe with unified discipling churches on the other five populated continents. Listed are the 12 targeted international cities that when a line is drawn connecting them forms a jagged circle – a redemptive **"crown of thorns"** – around the world: Santiago, Mexico City, Sao Paulo, London, Paris, Cairo, Johannesburg, Moscow, Chennai, Hong Kong, Manila and Sydney.

# The Crown Of Thorns Project

### The Plan For World Evangelism For The SoldOut Movement

*"But you will receive power when the Holy Spirit comes on you; and you will be my witnesses in Jerusalem, and in all Judea and Samaria, and to the ends of the earth."* Acts 1:8

## *"Jerusalem"* – Los Angeles

## *"Judea and Samaria"* – United States and Canada

***Judea:*** Las Vegas, Phoenix, Sacramento, San Diego and San Francisco

***Samaria:*** Albuquerque, Anchorage (2020), Ann Arbor (2020), Atlanta (2019), Boise (2020), Boston, Bridgeport (2019), Charlotte, Chicago, Columbus, Dallas/Ft. Worth, Denver, Eugene, Gainesville, Guam, Hilo, Honolulu, Houston, Kona, Miami/Ft. Lauderdale, Indianapolis (2019), Milwaukee, New York City, Orlando, **Philadelphia (2020)**, Portland, Seattle, Syracuse, Tampa, Toronto and Washington DC

### *"To The Ends Of The Earth"*

#### Phase One: Plant The Crown Of Thorns Churches

| | | |
|---|---|---|
| Santiago (2009) | Paris (2012) | Manila (2015) |
| London (2010) | Sydney (2014) | Lagos (2016) |
| São Paulo (2011) | Chennai (2014) | Dubai (2016) |
| Mexico City (2012) | Moscow (2015) | Hong Kong (2017) |

**Phase Two: Crown Of Thorns Churches Target Surrounding Nations' Capital Cities**
Abidjan, Amsterdam (2019), Auckland (2019), Bogotá, El Pocito, Johannesburg (2019), Kathmandu (2019), Kiev, Kinshasa, Lima (2019), Phnom Penh (2019), Port-au-Prince, Quito, Stockholm

**Phase Three: Each Capital City Church Evangelizes Their Nation**
Brazil (2), Davao (2019), Democratic Republic of Congo (4), England (2), Haiti (10), India (3), Ivory Coast (2), Mexico (2), Philippines (2), St. Petersburg (2020) Shenzhen (2019)
(Green – Church Plantings   Purple – Remnant Groups   Red – To Be Planted)

The Crown of Thorns Project in February 2019!

*It was so exciting that during the conference… that Joe and Kerry Willis of Brisbane, Australia solidified plans to move to LA for strengthening and further training… As He promised, our God is gathering a remnant from* ***"the farthest horizons."*** *(Nehemiah 1:8-9) It's happening!*

In 2016, through a series of events, the Spirit guided us to plant Lagos instead of Johannesburg as our pillar church for Africa, and Dubai instead of Cairo as our pillar church in the

113

Middle East. From the 2009 GLC to date, **The Crown of Thorns Project** has become a rallying vision for the Movement. Throughout the SoldOut Churches, disciples like me simply want to make a difference and change the world.

Rob Onekea and the author created a beautiful representation of Kip's masterful plan of the Crown of Thorns Project!

# GOD GATHERS FROM THE FARTHEST HORIZON

God has always worked through a *"remnant"* from the days of Noah to the present. Biblically, *"remnant"* is defined as the small group of *"survivors"* that have retained or returned to God's truths after most of God's people have not chosen this path. (Isaiah 10:20-22) Nehemiah prayed to God for the remnant, *"Remember the instruction you gave to your servant Moses saying, 'If you are unfaithful, I will scatter you among the nations, but if you return to me and obey my commands, then even if your exiled people are at the farthest horizon, I will gather them from there...'"* (Nehemiah 1:8-9) Who would disagree that the ICOC was *"scattered among the nations?"* Therefore, so exciting in our day, God is gathering His remnant from *"the farthest horizons"* into His New Movement!

When the Lord sent the McKeans to Portland in 2003, only 25 *"survivors"* gathered at that first Midweek Service. Yet this 25 through faith, forgiveness and discipling became the sold-out base to which God added. Interestingly, though the Portland Church was planted in 1991, they had never planted a single church until the McKeans arrived and were considered "small and relatively insignificant." Yet gathered that fateful Wednesday evening were the "remnant disciples" that became the seeds of leadership for God's New Movement. Among those attending that night were: Nick and Denise Bordieri, Tony and Therese Untalan, their daughter Coleen (Challinor) – the only faithful teen, Jeremy and Amy Ciaramella, Jay and Angie Hernandez, Michael and Michele Williamson, and Sarah Travis (Dimitry) – one of only four college students! Fascinatingly, all of these now "dynamic leaders in the SoldOut Movement" were "unknowns" to all the leaders of what remained of the ICOC. (1 Corinthians 1:26-30)

By March 2004, the Spirit brought to Portland from "their exile" working a secular job in St. Louis, the first former full-time ICOC family – Victor and Sonia Gonzalez and their 10 children. Victor Sr. was fired in LA, because his "leadership style" was "too much like Kip's." From 2004 to date, a thirsty remnant has come into the SoldOut Movement congregations finding *"living water"* – "the church they were baptized in!" Among the leaders – both former fulltime and non-fulltime – are: Chris and Kerri-Sue Adams, Erik and Michelle af Klint, Bolaji and Chinyere Akinfenwa, Alfredo and Alejandra Anuch, RD Baker, Evan and Kelly Bartholomew, Kyle Bartholomew, Cory Blackwell, Timur and Vika Butakov, John and Emma Causey, Jeremiah and Julie Clark, Chris and Sonja Chloupek, Ian and Margot Clague, Anthony and Elizabeth Eckels, Jim and Donna Fenton, Blaise and Patricia Feumba, Cecy Frazier, Hector and Adriana Gomez, Ronnie Gonzalez, Jacques and Jeanette Groenewald, Bill and Lisa Hamilton, Michael and Maria Hart, Kacie Jimenez, Peter and Lori Jordan, Slava and Lena Kapskiy, Tim and Lianne Kernan, Michael and Sharon Kirchner, Matthew and Marlo Lovacheff, Afa Maile, John and Anna Malnegro, Nimrod and Vis Malnegro, LuJack and Cathi Martinez, Jack and Jeanne McGee, Carlos and Lucy Mejia, Raul and Lynda Moreno, Micky and Lyly Ngungu, Ghislain & Debbie Normand, Gary and Cyndee Ochs, Rob and Burgandie Onekea, Roger and Kama Parlour and their children Joel and Brittany (Underhill), Jermaine and Stefanie Peacock, Gina Dela Pena, John and Bernie Pereda, Mike and Suzette Purdy, Raja and Debs Rajan, Joe and Mary Santos, Philippe and Prisca Scheidecker, Jay and Barb Shelbrack, Oleg and Aliona Sirotkin, Andrew and Patrique Smellie, Jenia and Julia Sobolev, Amadou and Angele Sountoura, Matt and Helen Sullivan, Dave and Jill Swann, Chris Teves, Renato and Marie Jose Tria, Salvador and Patricia Velasco, Alexey and Irina Vorozchenko, Lance and Connie Underhill and their sons – Mike and Joey, Rene and Anita Vermaat, Joe and Kerry Willis, Menno and Yuklin Zoutendijk, and Tracy and me.

Tim and Lianne Kernan "spied out the land"
with the McKeans in Paris in 2010!

In 2010, one of the most significant events was the coming of Cory Blackwell, the former World Sector Leader for the Middle East. Cory's placing membership (now he calls it his restoration) in November 2010 was such a balm for Kip's own wounds. Though the trauma of Cory's wife leaving the Lord over ten years before and the subsequent ostracization from all ICOC congregations had almost destroyed Cory's faith, Cory not only was reinstated Evangelist at the 2011 Global Leadership Conference, but now leads the Chicago

International Christian Church alongside his wonderful wife Jee. They have also been given Cory's former charge to once again evangelize the Middle East. (*City of Angels International Christian Church Bulletin – November 28, 2010 The Dream Never Dies*) Excitingly, since Cory became part of God's modern-day Movement, his daughter Avrie has become a very dynamic baptized disciple!

Cory and Kip in 1994!

When Cory Blackwell joined the
Movement, this was such an
encouragement to all
the remnant!

In June 2011, another valiant leader Blaise Feumba and his wife Patricia joined God's New Movement. Upon requesting to join the New Movement, Blaise expressed to Kip his sorrow for his signing the two letters against him in 2005. He apologized for his cowardice and was moved by Kip's unconditional forgiveness. This email to Kip is recorded in the *City of Angels International Christian Church Bulletin – June 19, 2011 The Glory Of The Second Temple:*

*Dear Kip,*

*I remembered those 10 minutes I spent with you in Seattle [at the 2005 ICOC Leadership Conference] wanting to understand what was going on in our family of churches at that moment. You told me you were going to start another movement compelled by the Spirit of God. At that*

119

*point, I wasn't sure that was the best thing to do, but after the churches in French Africa went through the same Satanic rebellion in 2007 [as the USA Churches in 2003], I understood what you meant in that room at the Seattle Conference... Most of what has been said about you and Elena has been said about Patricia and me on a very smaller scale. But the pain and the sufferings we have been through were used by the Lord to draw us closer to His heart through countless nights of tears and grief in His purifying hands.*

*We survived by God's grace and kept preaching the Gospel for which I have been called. From a church [which I once led] of over 2,000 members in Abidjan, [Ivory Coast], a band of about 20 courageous disciples followed Patricia and me for the start of a new planting. We were all resolved to follow the clouds and not the crowds convinced that the church we have given our youth for was dead with politics and deceit. This was the new game played by the shepherds in the ICOC for power and influence. Without any support from men, we grew from 20 to over 100 in two years, as well as sending out a new planting to Hiré, Ivory Coast, which now numbers 30 disciples...*

*I want to use this time to let you know that I am sorry for the letters that I signed against you in 2005, because I was not courageous enough to stand against the crowds. I did this against my conscience, but of this I do not blame anyone other than myself. Please forgive me brother because I have sinned against the Lord with a band of brothers who wanted to kill their "father" to take his position. We did not learn from David who understood that God hated rebellion against Saul no matter how badly Saul had treated him. I have no hatred in my heart against my former friends. In fact, I have resolved to pray for them every day begging the Lord to draw them back to once again be close to His heart...*

*At this time, I can't think of another captain I would like to pursue this with. I have watched you over the past three years. Your deeds speak of God's mighty hand on you. No matter what you have been through you are still standing stronger than ever for Jesus and for His mission to see this lost world evangelized in one generation. You have proven yourself worthy to be followed as you follow Christ. Here am I... with a burning desire to save as many souls as possible. I need you in my life. Our love to Elena.*

*Blaise and Patricia Feumba*

Blaise and Patricia Feumba with their three children –
Helena, Odelia and Yoel!

With the Feumbas' coming, two more "remnant churches" were added to the Movement in Ivory Coast – Abidjan and Hiré. These groups remembered and appreciated that Blaise and Patricia had served in the ICOC as GSL's (Geographic Sector Leaders) and brought to the Gospel to them, as well as all 22 ICOC congregations in the 14 nations of French-speaking Africa. The Feumbas were likewise reinstated at the 2011 GLC to be Evangelist and Women's Ministry Leader. They now joyfully serve the Lord as full-time servants in the North Region of the City of Angels Church,

121

also overseeing French-speaking Africa and the work in Hispaniola.

As stated before, Kip's conviction is that the ultimate reason that the first Movement failed to evangelize all nations was the lack of grace, mercy and forgiveness in his leadership, as well as in other leaders' lives. Therefore, whenever someone is restored or places membership at the City of Angels Church, Kip often personally leads the song, *We Love You With The Love Of The Lord*. Also, similar to the brothers greeting Paul at Rome, but unique to the SoldOut Movement is the "chorus of sold-out disciples" who gather at their city's airport to greet fellow disciples from anywhere around the world with the song, *We Love You With The Love Of The Lord!* This is practiced by all SoldOut Movement Churches on all six populated continents, as this hymn has become the anthem of God's New Movement trumpeting for all to hear that this "second time" to *"love the Lord with all your heart and with all your soul and with all our mind and with all our strength" and "to love your neighbor as yourself"* will be the preeminent teachings!

# THE NEW MOVEMENT MULTIPLIES

In August at the 2010 Global Leadership Conference entitled EXODUS, the second Crown Of Thorns City – London – now led dynamically by Michael and Michele Williamson was sent out!

Michael and Michele Williamson on the London Eye, which overlooked Big Ben and Parliament!

The Moscow Mission Team Leaders – Oleg and Aliona Sirotkin with their precious daughters Sophia and Lidia in 2010!

The third Crown Of Thorns Church Planting – **São Paulo** was sent-out by the Spirit at the 2011 Global Leadership

Conference entitled, **THE CALLING**. This noble effort is courageously led by Raul and Lynda Moreno.

Raul and Lynda Moreno were the gallant
leaders of the São Paulo Mission Team!

The theme for the 2012 Global Leadership Conference was **CHOSEN – SPIRITUAL LEADERSHIP IN THE DAYS OF THE JUDGES**. A historic five mission teams were sent out by the hand of God: Boston, San Francisco and Orlando, as well as the fourth and fifth Crown Of Thorns Plantings: Mexico City and Paris. Paris was inspirationally led by Tim and Lianne Kernan, French-speaking Canadians who came to the first Portland Jubilee and later formed the London Remnant Group! As of today, they have the great honor to lead the City of Angels International Christian Church!

On a special note, it was one of the great "joys of our lives" for Tracy and me to lead the Washington DC Church beginning in 2012! June 2013 marked a historic event – as we saw a first in the SoldOut Movement: The sending out of the Denver Mission Team – the first third generation church as LA sent out DC and in turn DC sent out Denver! Of course, the Lord always blesses those who truly give up everything, and so He gave the then 100-member DC Church a big hug blessing our International Day Sunday Services on the lawn of the National Mall with attendances of 508 in 2013 and 646 in 2014!

The author preached before a crowd of 508 on the lawn of the National Mall in 2013!

# THE FOUNDING OF THE INTERNATIONAL COLLEGE OF CHRISTIAN MINISTRIES

Every major "Christian denomination" in the world has established their own seminary to formalize their doctrines and to train their ministers. On two different occasions in our former fellowship – in Boston in the early 80's with the "Boston School of World Missions" and in LA in the early 90's with the "Los Angeles International School of Ministry" – Kip sought to establish an accredited school. Sadly, the leadership of the ICOC never came to a consensus on the curriculum in order to establish a school where degrees were recognized. Being *"brought to complete unity"* (John 17:23) with the founding of the International College of Christian Ministries (ICCM), the Central Leadership Council and the church leaders worldwide in God's New Movement fulfilled Jesus prayer in the Garden of Gethsemane to let the world know He has sent us!

One of the first goals of the ICCM was to recognize those who already serve as Evangelists and Women's Ministry Leaders by formally granting to each of them a well-earned BA in Ministry Degree at the 2013 Global Leadership Conference! So, at the 2013 Global Leadership Conference entitled PROPHETS AND KINGS – THEY LONGED TO SEE WHAT "WE" SEE, we all *"stood in awe of [our] God"* as 94 individuals received their BA, Master's or Doctorate Degrees!

Michael Kirchner - Chairman of the Board
of Regents of the ICCM – introduced
the Processional for the historic
First ICCM Graduation!

As the Processional began Wagner's *Ride*
of the Valkyries was played!

"We were like men AND WOMEN
*who dreamed!"* (Psalm 126:1)

"Young men saw visions; old men
dreamed dreams!" (Acts 2:17)

The Latin motto of the ICCM came from
John 1:14: "Venia et Veritas" which
means "Grace and Truth!"

*The 2013 GLC City of Angels Church Bulletin* read:

*It is with great pleasure that we welcome you to the 2013
Inaugural Commencement Ceremony of the International
College of Christian Ministries (ICCM)! This "dream
become reality" was made possible because the Lord
answered our prayers on August 16, 2012, as the*

*California Bureau of Postsecondary Education approved our application for the founding of the ICCM. We received the "Verification of Exempt Status" which allows the ICCM to grant accredited Bachelor's, Master's and Doctorate Degrees in Ministry according to "our" Biblical doctrines and standards.*

*This "school of prophets" (2 Kings 2:3, 5) is not a substitute for Jesus' plan to train ministers by walking with them side-by-side for a period of years. (Mark 3:13) The SoldOut Movement Leadership believes that "our appointed ministers" – Evangelists, Women's Ministry Leaders, Shepherds, Shepherdesses and Administrators – are among the best trained and most effective in all Christendom. What we have lacked hitherto is the vehicle to accredit the robust and dynamic course of training that our leaders already undertake, while augmenting our present efforts with more classroom oriented Biblical studies.*

All of the ICCM Degree recipients recognized the
historic magnitude of the Commencement!

*The European Degree System – Bachelor's, Master's and Doctorate Degrees – has been one of the most successful European cultural exports in history. The doctorate (Latin: docio) originated in Medieval Europe as a license to teach (Latin: licentia docendi) at a Medieval*

130

*university. Its roots can be traced to the early church when the term "doctor" referred to the Apostles, Church Fathers and other Christian authorities who taught and interpreted the Bible. This academic program is now present in almost every part of the world – even in China and Saudi Arabia, countries which are not viewed as being "pro-Western."*

*This Degree System has been fully embraced globally, as the most legitimate indication of competency and qualification in a professional field. Today, we are able to accord these very high honors to our students as we recognize years of training and diligent work for the advancement of the Gospel all over the world in this generation.*

*To found a college with the European Degree System, there must be at its head an individual holding the Doctorate Degree. Therefore, today Thomas W. "Kip" McKean II will be awarded the Doctorate Degree (D.Min.) for his years of preaching, teaching, training and building churches around the world. This is not to mention his widespread writings as a scholar and theologian. His formal training and experiences at University of Florida in Speech Communications (High Honors), as well as at Eastern Baptist Theological Seminary and the Harding Graduate School of Religion have enriched his leadership. Kip humbly serves as the President of the ICCM.*

*Others on the "ICCM Leadership Team" are Chris Adams (BA – Yale University; MS – Long Island University; M.Min. – ICCM), who diligently serves as our Vice President and the Dean of Academics, as well as Elena McKean (BS – University of Florida; M.Min. – ICCM), who nobly serves as the Dean of Women as well as a professor. With 36 years of full-time ministry, as well as being born in Cuba, Elena will provide great insight into the challenges of building a college of diversity.*

131

*Our Chairman of the Board of Regents that oversees the ICCM is the Administrator for the SoldOut Movement, Michael Kirchner (BA – University of Iowa; MBA – University of Minnesota). Also serving on the Board of Regents are Tim Kernan (BA – ICCM; M.Min. – ICCM), Andrew Smellie (BS – Cornell University; MA – Cornell University), and Helen Sullivan (BA – Stanford University; MHA – Stanford University). Pray for the entire ICCM Leadership Team, as the ICCM is a "work in progress."*

*The ICCM is dedicated to the glory of Jesus Christ hence our motto (in Latin) comes from John 1:14, Venia et Veritas – "Grace and Truth." [Latin was the "lingua franca," the language adopted as the common language between speakers who had different native languages, especially for the "intelligentsia." Therefore, it continues to be used for college mottos to this day.]*

*Let us consider the ICCM's future with the words of John F. Kennedy, 35th President of the United States of America: "The energy, the faith, the devotion which we bring to this endeavor will light our country and all who serve it – and the glow from that fire can truly light the world."*

*Thank you for joining us for this momentous event, and congratulations to all those who are receiving degrees today!"*

*The ICCM Leadership Team*

There was such a sense of honor, integrity and humility in the air as Kip fell to one knee while bowing his head as Michael Kirchner – Chairman of the Board of Regents – "hooded" Kip deservingly awarding him the Doctorate of Ministry Degree! (D.Min.) This single moment brought a thunderous and prolonged standing ovation of the almost 2,000 in attendance!

Kip received the first ICCM Doctorate of Ministry Degree!

Kip delivered a stirring Commencement Address!

Then, Kip delivered the following memorable address:

*Sir Francis Bacon in 1597 wrote, "Knowledge is power." Yet let the word go forth on this historic day that 'Scriptural knowledge' gives access to divine power but only obedience to the Scriptures gives eternal life – our hope for all mankind.*

*John 1:14 reads, **"The Word became flesh and made His dwelling among us. We have seen His glory, the glory of the One and Only, who came from the Father, full of grace and truth."** This is the theme Scripture for the ICCM. From it comes the Latin Motto of our college Venia et Veritas – "Grace and Truth." This college honors our Savior Jesus Christ by augmenting the already excellent training of our ministers and women ministry leaders. In fact, our ministers and women's ministry leaders are among the best trained in the world.*

*Today is historic! Our former fellowship in the early 80's established the Boston School of World Missions, yet a degree path could not be established. In the 90's, we established the Los Angeles International School of Ministry and again no consensus could be reached for a*

134

*degree path. Today is miraculous as we witness the fulfillment that this present "remnant temple" has become more glorious than our "former temple." And to God be the glory!*

Then Kip turned to the 90 brothers and sisters who had walked across the stage receiving their BA Diplomas. He charged them, "Please stand, all BA Degree Candidates of the historic Class of 2013! By the authority vested in me by God, by the ICCM Regents, and by the Great State of California, I duly confer upon you the Bachelor of Ministry Degree! Congratulations! You may move your tassels from right to left!"

Admiral McKean was "front and center" at the presentation of the 90 BA of Ministry Degree Recipients and for Kip's hooding to receive his Doctorate Degree!

# The International College of
# Christian Ministries

The President and Board of Regents acting on recommendation of the Faculty has conferred upon

## Ronald Caleb Harding, Jr.

### The Degree of Bachelor of Arts in Ministry

And have granted all the rights and privileges thereto pertaining. In witness thereof, by authority duly committed to us, we have hereunder placed our names and the seal of the college on this the fourth day of August in the year of our Lord two thousand and thirteen at Los Angeles, California.

Thomas W. McKean III
President and Founder

Elena G. McKean
Dean of Women

Christopher T. Adams
Vice President

Michael J. Kirchner
Chairman - Board of Regents

The highlight of the 2013 GLC for the author was
the ICCM Commencement!

For Ron and Tracy Harding, receiving
recognition for their ministry training,
made their physical families so proud!

Following came the awarding of the Master's in Ministry Degrees by "hooding" Chris Adams, Tim Kernan and Elena McKean!

Congratulations to Elena in earning the Master's of Ministry Degree from the ICCM where she serves as the Dean of Women and as a Professor!

To conclude, Kip shared his vision that an Evangelist awarded the ICCM Master's Degree will be able "to open" an extension campus in his city! As of 2018, the ICCM-LA has 10 extension campuses: Columbus, Lagos, Manila, Miami, New York City, Portland, San Francisco, São Paulo, Toronto and Washington DC!

# 2014 THE YEAR OF PRAYER

I am so encouraged Kip selected my suggestion in making 2014 **The Year of Prayer** for the SoldOut Movement. At the City of Angels Church Winter Workshop – attended by church leaders from around the world – Jesus' vision for the church was embraced, *"My house will be a house of prayer for all nations."* (Mark 11:17) Excitingly, through the prayers and hard work of the saints, the Spirit planted new discipling congregations in 2014 in: Gainesville, Florida; Sydney, Australia; Houston, Texas; Toronto, Canada; Dallas/Ft. Worth, Texas; and Chennai, India!

The heroic Sydney Mission Team!

The Crown of Thorns Project was first presented in August 2009. Amazingly, with the plantings of Sydney and Chennai in 2014, eight of the 12 Crown of Thorns Project Cities had been planted in just five years! This powerful moving of the Spirit was evident to all!

In 2014, Kip preached on several occasions that "challenges" are viewed as "problems" when we have little faith and "opportunities" when we pray and act in faith. (Mark 11:23-24) Indeed, there were many "opportunities" that year! As in the late 1980's and because the New Movement had likewise grown so rapidly, the McKeans once again were "feeling the challenges" of being spread "too thin" by discipling too many couples and churches. They realized that the time had come to "focus on a few" by selecting World Sector Leaders (WSL) for the SoldOut Movement. After months of prayer, the World Sector Leaders were formally introduced at the Sunday morning service of the 2014 Global Leadership Conference – ZION'S DREAMERS.

Raja and Debs Rajan and the 14 Paid Interns of the
Chennai International Christian Church in 2014!

At the WSL's very first meeting together on Wednesday morning August 7th, Kip delivered the message, Jesus The Savior Of The World. Immediately following, the WSL Couples shared communion. As each person broke the unleavened bread, the individual held it up and pledged to the group, "We are family." Then before drinking the cup that signifies the shedding of Jesus' blood at His death, the person added to the pledge, "To the end." Remembering that a lack of grace, mercy and humility were the downfall of our former fellowship, "We are family to the end" quickly became a rallying cry and in fact a "shibboleth" for the entire Movement.

Wooden challises were given to each World Sector
Leader Couple inscribed with their vow at their
first Communion, "We are family…
to the end."

Let me introduce the SoldOut Movement World Sector
Leaders as of 2018:

Cory and Jee Blackwell
MIDDLE EAST and MIDWEST USA

Tim, Lianne, Junior and David Kernan
PACIFIC RIM, WESTERN US and CANADA

Raul, Lynda, Felipe and Bella Moreno
CENTRAL and SOUTH AMERICA
and SOUTH USA

Andrew, Patrique, Naomi and the young prophet Isaiah Smellie!
AFRICA and MID-ATLANTIC USA

Oleg, Aliona, Sophia and Lidia Sirotkin
EURASIA (RUSSIAN COMMONWEALTH)

Matt and Helen Sullivan
SOUTH ASIA and EASTERN USA

Michael and Michele Williamson
EUROPE

144

Joe, Kerry, Ally and Luke Willis
AUSTRAL-CHINA

Nick and Denise Bordieri
MOVEMENT SHEPHERDING COUPLE
(Global Directors of MERCY*worldwide*)

Michael and Sharon Kirchner
MOVEMENT ADMINISTRATION and LAW

Tony and Therese Untalan
MOVEMENT SHEPHERDING COUPLE
(Global Overseers of Shepherding Couples)

The 2014 GLC had many highlights including the Second Commencement of the ICCM. The stirring Wagner classic *Ride Of The Valkyries* was once again played for the procession of the ICCM Faculty, Board and Graduates! Then a total of 57 BA Degrees were awarded in four different tracks for the first time: 21 were presented with BA Degrees in Ministry; three were given BA Degrees in Ministry and Administration; five received BA Degrees in Ministry and Charitable Services; and 28 earned BA Degrees in Ministry and Shepherding! Then Tim Kernan spoke on The ICCM And The European Degree System. Elena – our Dean of Women – followed up with the enlightening presentation of The Equal Opportunity For Sisters In The ICCM. Following this, three Master of Arts in Ministry Degrees were awarded to: Kyle Bartholomew, Lianne Kernan and Andrew Smellie; and then, the Master of Arts in Ministry and Administration Degree was awarded to Michael Kirchner!

The "hooding" of Andrew Smellie as he received
his Master's Degree!

Following came a moment that all of us will cherish for a long time: Dr. Tim Kernan "was hooded" and given the prestigious Doctorate of Ministry Degree!

Dr. Tim Kernan delivering an address on the History of the European Degree System!

The ICCM Faculty, Staff and Board of Regents in 2014!

**ZION'S DREAMERS** focused on prayer, missions and the "Five Core Convictions Of The SoldOut Movement" built on the foundation of Jesus being our resurrected Messiah. The fact that all of our members in every church hold these five core convictions have made the New Movement so much more unified and loving than our former Movement. Here are the five core convictions that divided the ICOC from the Mainline and then likewise divided the SoldOut

Movement from what was left of the ICOC when they returned to a more "Mainline theology:"

1. **All Scripture Inspired By God – Building A Bible Church**
   (2 Timothy 3:14-17)

2. **Where The Bible Speaks We Are Silent, And Where The Bible Is Silent We Speak**
   (Genesis 2:19; 1 Corinthians 10:23)

3. **The Church Is Composed Of Only Sold-out Disciples In Discipling Relationships**
   (Matthew 28:18-20; Acts 11:26; Colossians 1:28-29)

4. **A Central Leadership With A Central Leader Is God's Plan**
   (Numbers 27:15-18; Acts 15:19-24; 1 Corinthians 4:15-17)

5. **The Evangelization Of Nations In A Generation Is God's Will**
   (Colossians 1:6, 23; 1 Timothy 2:3-4; 1 Timothy 3:16; 1 Timothy 4:10; 2 Timothy 4:17)

Since the 2014 GLC was "Livestreamed" into 52 countries, this forthright address of the SoldOut Movement's convictions drew several remnant disciples to join the New Movement around the world. Of special note, the Jeddah (Saudi Arabia) Remnant Group was formed from those that watched the GLC Livestream. However, it also exposed "contempt and disunity" in a few "remnant" disciples, who left our fellowship after the GLC still believing in congregational autonomy and not central leadership. (Deuteronomy 17:12-13) Yet in all of this, God was sovereign, and His will was done. Through these challenging events, He graciously blessed the SoldOut Movement with the "opportunity" to be *"brought to complete unity to let the world know [that God] loved them."* (John 17:23)

149

The 2014 Global Leadership Conference!

Kip's commitment to follow Jesus' blueprint of His First Century Movement has led to another unique aspect of the SoldOut Movement – The Crown of Thorns Council. The World Sector Leaders of the SoldOut Movement parallel Jesus' Twelve. The Crown of Thorns Council parallels the 70 (or 72) of Luke 10. Jesus was never "random" in the use of numbers. In selecting the 12 Apostles, He was signaling to the Jews that a new Kingdom was being created. The physical nation of Israel came from the 12 sons of Jacob; spiritual Israel would come from the 12 Apostles.

Luke 10:1 reads, *"After this the Lord appointed [70] others and sent them two by two ahead of Him to every town…"* Kip is convinced (though not dogmatic) that it is "70" – not "72" as some versions have – that formed the second group of preachers Jesus commissioned, as the number "70" for the Jew is very special and stands for human leadership and judgment. Consider that there were 70 nations that composed the whole world in the "Table of Nations" in Genesis 10-11. As well, Moses selected 70 elders to lead with him. (Exodus 24:1) Historically, 70 men translated the oldest Greek version of the Old Testament called the Septuagint – Latin for 70. Notably, the Jewish Sanhedrin of Jesus' day was composed of 70 men. In essence, Kip believes the 70 of Luke 10 are the "Apostles" of 1

Corinthians 15:7 and were a part of the 120 of Acts 1:15. Most importantly, he has deep convictions that the appointing of the 70 was Jesus signaling the evangelization of the nations, as the Table of Nations in Genesis suggests. Whatever your convictions about whether it was 70 or 72 is fine. The point is that Kip realized the absolute need of a second larger group of preachers to not only preach the Word, but to promote a greater unity. Therefore, to this day, the Crown of Thorns Council (with whom the WSL meet) oversees the evangelization of the nations.

As answered prayers have propelled God's Movement to greater heights, perhaps the greatest "opportunity" for God to work directly in the McKeans' lives came in April 2014. It was at this time that Elena was diagnosed by her doctor with an early stage of bone cancer (Multiple Myeloma), which the medical community views as ultimately incurable. This diagnosis was made because of a highly elevated calcium level in Elena's blood, as well as cancer markers. Cancer markers are simply proteins produced by the cancer cells or a protein produced by the white blood cells when they attack the cancer cells.

At first, Kip and Elena were stunned by the news. They shared with their family and closest brothers and sisters asking them all to pray for Elena's recovery. The McKeans prayed and fasted through "juicing." After going through more tests in May and June, on June 11th, Elena's oncologist (cancer doctor), who is the head of the department, greeted the McKeans with a big grin, sat down on the examination table, and said, "Never in all my years of practice have I seen anything like this! Your calcium is back to normal and your cancer markers are gone!" Knowing Kip and Elena were in the ministry, he then added, "I'm sure that you both prayed a lot!" In fact, this was very true! Though Elena has shared she is not afraid to die, inspired by Hezekiah's prayer, Elena prayed to live 20 more years so that she could see the world evangelized!

151

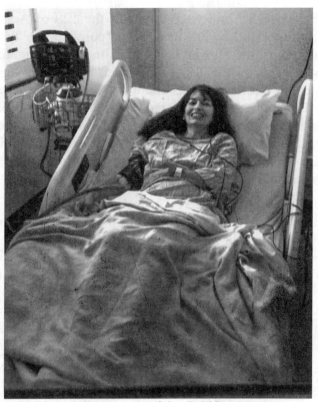

God heard the prayers of the SoldOut Movement
and cured Elena of cancer!

One last splendid "opportunity" for God to work in 2014 through the SoldOut Movement was the raising of the funds to be able to accomplish the seven church plantings that calendar year while sustaining our already productive efforts in the third world. Remarkably, the collective weekly giving of the SoldOut Movement Churches was $85,000 per week. Amazingly, in The Year of Prayer, the sold-out disciples of the SoldOut Movement through prayer, fasting and creative fundraising sacrificially gave to God another $2,000,000 for missions giving us *"more than we could ask or imagine"* to accomplish all that God put on our hearts to do for His glory! (Ephesians 3:20-21) Truly, 2014 is remembered as The Year of Answered Prayers!

# 2015 THE YEAR OF MATURITY

Highlights for 2015 – the thrilling **Year of Maturity** – included the planting of two more Crown of Thorns Cities – Moscow and Manila! With the escalating tension between America and Russia, being in a unified Movement gave God all the more glory. In Ephesians 2:14, Paul describes this amazing aspect of the Kingdom, *"For He Himself is our peace who has made the two one and has destroyed the barrier, the dividing wall of hostility… His purpose was to create in Himself one new man out of the two, thus making peace, and in this one body to reconcile both of them to God through the cross by which he put to death their hostility."* (Ephesians 2:14-16) The gathering of the Moscow Mission Team was unique. In 2012, Kip asked Oleg and Aliona Sirotkin – who were leading the Kiev (Ukraine) Remnant Group – to come and train in Los Angeles. Kip and Elena understood that remnant ministry couples needed a time of strengthening – even up to a year – in order to have the closeness to God and the spiritual strength to handle the rigors and pressures of day-to-day ministry. (2 Corinthians 11:28) As well, Oleg and Aliona had to perfect their English in order to lead in America. This too was a focus of their first year in LA.

During the second and third years of the Sirotkins' training, Kip collectively asked the disciples in the Kiev and Moscow Remnant Groups to come to LA's South Region for as long as they could support themselves. (The South Region was the McKeans' "home base" and where the Sirotkins led.) Incredibly, a total of 15 disciples – about half from Kiev and the other half from Moscow – paid for their tickets to come to America and supported themselves while they lived there. Some could only support themselves for a month; a few of them were able to stay for a year. Afterward, they returned to Moscow to prayerfully await the time of the Sirotkins' coming.

The miraculous Moscow Mission Team!

Excitingly, during the Sirotkins' stay, there oldest daughter Sophia was baptized in 2014! It was in the midst of Elena fighting cancer that she counted the cost with Sophia on Monday night, May 19th. Sophia was baptized the following day in the Pacific Ocean after Staff Meeting by Oleg and Aliona! Their adopted daughter Lidia was baptized at the 2016 GLC! Indeed, just like the Sirotkins, all around the world whole families are being united in Christ!

Sofia was baptized on May 20, 2014!

So sacrificially in December of 2014, every single member of the Moscow Mission Team again paid for their tickets to fly from Moscow to LA in order to be at the Send-Off Service on December 14th! The following day the Sirotkins flew back to Moscow with their mission team! The glorious Inaugural Service was on February 1, 2015.

The Inaugural Invitation to the Swiss Hotel for
February 1, 2015!

Kip shared with me that when he awoke very early that morning, there was a blistering snow storm! In his quiet time, he fell to his knees praying for God to stop the storm. (I am sure the entire Moscow Mission Team was doing the same!) At 8:00AM, Kip walked to the Swiss Hotel Conference Center. He shared that the snow was several inches deep and the wind was so strong that the snow was flying by him sideways. By 10:00AM, the snow stopped. By 11:00AM – the planned time for the beginning of the service – Kip stepped outside and even saw some blue sky through the clouds! Amazingly, the 17 on the mission team were joined by 29 in the remnant group and God blessed their Inaugural Service with an attendance of 227 and two baptisms!

God answered the prayers of the disciples by stopping
the snow storm just in time for Oleg Sirotkin to
preach to the 227 that God gathered for the
Moscow ICC Inaugural Service!

To welcome everyone to the Inaugural Service, Kip read Ephesians 2:14-17 and said, "Today we gather not as citizens of Russia, Ukraine or America, but as citizens in the Kingdom of God. We come together not as Russian Christians, Ukrainian Christians or American Christians, but as Global Disciples!" As of 2018, the Moscow Church has 130 disciples, as the disciples have persevered through this time where it is against Russian law to share your faith. In fact, the surging hostilities toward Christianity were probably responsible for the entire Moscow Teen Ministry being taken into custody by the police for singing too loudly at their devotional in 2016. Though Russia and the Ukraine are united in language, but deeply divided by politics, the newly planted Kiev Church has still grown to almost 50 disciples!

Four months later, the Manila Mission Team was sent out from LA led by Kyle and Joan Bartholomew! For the record, the Manila Remnant Group was initiated in late 2012 by one woman who took her stand against the lukewarmness and false doctrine taught in our former fellowship. Her name is

Gina Dela Pena. When she stood up for the truth, she was unjustly disfellowshipped; yet John and Anna Malnegro soon joined her.

Very interestingly, when the McKeans led the original Manila Mission Team in 1989, there were 26 disciples on the team. Kip selected the Makati Intercontinental Hotel for the Inaugural Service of the Metro Manila Christian Church in 1989. God blessed them with 260 in attendance! So incredible was that for the Inaugural Service of the Metro Manila International Christian Church on June 7, 2015, Kip and Elena gave the Welcome in the very same hotel in the very same room as in 1989! This time God blessed the eight on the mission team and the 39 in the Manila Remnant Group with 306 in attendance! Sadly, the Intercontinental Hotel was torn down in late 2016. As of 2018, the Manila Church has grown to nearly 300 disciples and has sent out their first mission team to the second largest city in the Philippines – Cebu! The Cebu Mission Team was led by John and Anna Malnegro! The Cebu Church now numbers 50 disciples! Lord willing, the Davao Mission Team will be sent out in June 2019 at the Pacific Rim Missions Conference!

The Intercontinental Hotel in Metro Manila was
the site of the Inaugural Services in
both 1989 and 2015!

For Kip and Elena, another highlight of June 2015 was the First African Missions Conference held in Abidjan, Ivory Coast! This effort to plant by reconstruction the Abidjan Church with only sold-out disciples was led by Blaise and Patricia Feumba. The remnant group of 100 disciples had the cost counted with each member. Astoundingly, on the Sunday of the African Missions Conference there were 498 in attendance from 11 different African Nations! They closed out the service with 12 glorious baptisms!

At the conclusion of the First African Missions Conference, a new custom came into the SoldOut Movement: While singing *There Is A Joy* a conga line formed which circled the entire room!

Another highlight of the Year of Maturity was Elena McKean receiving her Doctorate Degree at the ICCM Commencement Ceremony during the 2015 GLC entitled, **SAVIOR OF THE WORLD!** Her dissertation was on what she has named the "Women's Elevation Section" of the Book of Luke found in chapters seven and eight. Her inspiring title was *ELEVATE – Jesus' Global Revolution For Women.*

Livestream of the 2015 GLC was broadcast to 69 different nations!

This scholarly dissertation contained a number of insights about Jesus' relationship with women. Among these insights is that women were in ***"His company"*** (Luke 8:2 MSG) and

159

were there because like the Apostles, they were selected by Jesus to be with Him. Unknown to many disciples is that Jesus followed the practice of the rabbis of that day of selecting men for Him to teach. His uniqueness was that Jesus chose women as well! That is why the first greeting given to the resurrected Jesus by Mary of Magdalene was "Rabboni!" She saw Jesus as her mentor just like the men did!

Elena inspired the audience that Jesus was
uniquely a Rabbi to men AND women!

Another insight in the Elena's book came from Micah 6:4 which talks about the leadership of Israel in the desert, *"I brought you up out of Egypt and redeemed you from the land of slavery. I sent Moses to lead you, also Aaron and Miriam."* Elena had a terrific insight that God for His earthly family – those in the Exodus Movement – needed a female influence just like human families need a mother's influence. Generally speaking, women are gentler and kinder than their male counterparts. Therefore, one of the reasons that "conservative churches" – such as the Mainline Church of Christ – become rigid and harsh in *"life and doctrine"* is that women have no influence and really no presence in the leadership of the church. To be clear, Elena does not believe that a woman should have authority over a man or that she can be an evangelist. She believes as the Bible teaches, that the women disciple the women. (Titus 2:4-5) That said,

160

women should have a voice in the church that helps to build a congregation that is loving, merciful and kind. I now fully understand why Kip has always had the wives of the Evangelists attend all the Staff Meetings; Kip like Jesus called women to be in *"his company."*

For a celebration party after the GLC, Kip had a speciality cake made in honor of Elena receiving her Doctorate Degree and of her 60th Birthday!

Elena received her Doctorate Degree at the same
Commencement that Rebecca Rico
Gray was Valedictorian for
the Class of 2015!

To close the year, a historic event occurred at the Christmas
Service in December. Kip and Elena – sensing the Spirit's
call to minister to the Crown of Thorns Churches and the key
churches in America – handed over the leadership of their
beloved City of Angels Church to Tim and Lianne Kernan.
At this tearful service, Kip shared like Paul about "his"
Timothy, *"I have no one else like him… But you know that
Timothy has proved himself, because as a son with his
father he has served with me in the work of the Gospel."*
(Philippians 2:20-22)

The City of Angels Church Staff honored and sent off the
McKeans to the mission field!

The McKeans hand off the City of Angels Church at
2015 Christmas Service to their beloved
son and daughter in the faith –
Tim and Lianne Kernan!

# 2016 THE YEAR OF FAMILY

The theme Scripture for The Year of Family was 1 Peter 5:8-9, *"Be self-controlled and alert. Your enemy the devil prowls around like a roaring lion looking for someone to devour. Resist him, standing firm in the faith, because you know that your FAMILY THROUGHOUT THE WORLD is undergoing the same kind of sufferings."* The Year of Family was perhaps best expressed in the seven Geographic Missions Conferences that were held outside of the United States. So many disciples cannot afford to come to the Jerusalem of the Movement – Los Angeles – for the Annual Global Leadership Conferences. For most, this is financially prohibitive and for many it is also not possible to obtain visas to come to the United States. So as Kip said in explaining the need for Geographic Conferences, "If Moses cannot go to the mountain, then bring the mountain to Moses!" And of course, just as in the Old Testament Scriptures, the mountain is the Kingdom of God!

Kip preached the close-out message for the Pacific Rim Missions Conference - HEROES IN THE FAITH!

In February, was the Second Brazil Missions Conference in São Paulo, where the Spirit sent out their first mission team to Rio de Janeiro! (The Brazil Missions Conference is now called the South American Missions Conference with the host site alternating between São Paulo and Santiago.)

164

Several of the young men that Raul trained for the
ministry were able to meet Kip and Elena for
the very first time and at the First Brazil
Missions Conference in São Paulo!

The following weekend was the First Latin American Missions Conference in Mexico City! That Sunday was the sending out of the Bogota (Colombia) Mission Team! In May was the First Eurasian Missions Conference in Moscow! In June, we celebrated the First Pacific Rim Missions Conference, as well as the Second African Missions Conference (AMC) which was held this time in Lagos!

Sunday of the AMC was the Inaugural Service of the Lagos International Christian Church, which was the planting of our Tenth Crown of Thorns Congregation! Amazingly, God gave them an incredible 155 in attendance with three baptisms! In their first year, the 11 on the mission team, joined by eight in the remnant group, grew to almost 100 disciples! In October was the European Missions Conference in London, where they sent out the Birmingham (England) Mission Team! Then in November was the First South Asia Missions Conference in Chennai, India where 12 were baptized on Sunday and their first mission team was sent out to Bangalore, India!

The First Latin American Missions Conference in Mexico
City was entitled, **THE GREAT COMMISSION**!

Oleg Sirotkin translated Kip at the First Eurasian
Missions Conference in Moscow!

During the Pacific Rim Missions Conference, a special
MERCY Event was held at the Asociacion
De Damas Filipinas Orphange!

The Second African Missions Confernce in Lagos
provided the McKeans with the opportunity to
work side-by-side with their dear son and
daughter in the faith - Andrew
and Patrique!

The day after the European Missions Conference ended,
the McKeans met with Williamsons and the four new
Region Leader Couples for the London Church!

As with all the Geographic Missions Conferences,
the First South Asia Missions Conference
had tremendous cultural dances!

Without question, the Spirit has guided the timing and
planting of all our churches, especially the Crown of Thorns
Congregations! In early 2015, Kip received a Facebook

message from Benedict Atason, who was a Mainline Church of Christ Preacher in Umuahia, Nigeria. He humbly requested to join the Movement as he had been reading about it on the internet for several years. As is Kip's custom, he tested Benedict's sincerity and depth of conviction by asking him to attend the First African Missions Conference (AMC) in Abidjan.

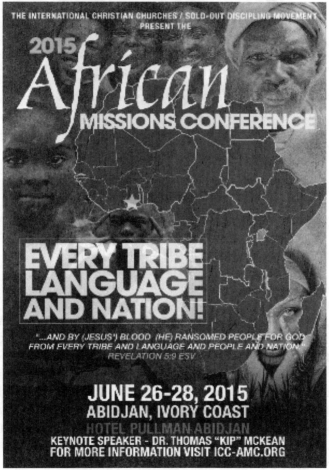

The First African Missions Conference was entitled,
Every Tribe, Language and Nation!

Kip enjoys preaching in emerging
countries like Nigeria, as people
are far more in touch with
their need for a savior!

Kip was pleasantly surprised when Benedict came as it required him travelling in a bus through four nations! At the conference, Kip, Andrew Smellie and Blaise Feumba studied with Benedict about his conversion and the core convictions of the SoldOut Movement. Interestingly, Benedict was born the same year – in 1954 as Kip and was baptized in the same year 1972! After three days of studies, they determined Benedict's baptism to be valid and Benedict was wholehearted in his embracing of the SoldOut Movement Core Convictions!

At the First AMC, a whole day was set aside for a
special MERCY Event to feed the poor!

After the AMC, Benedict travelled to Lagos to reach out to his son Goodhope, who also was a Mainline Church of Christ preacher. After studying with him, Goodhope took his stand for the truth and a remnant group of eight was formed! A few months later, Benedict visited the City of Angels Church in LA. It was at this point that he talked to Kip and Andrew about changing the Crown of Thorns target city from Johannesburg to Lagos. He cited the fact that Lagos is the largest city in all of Africa at 21 million and that Nigeria has the largest population of any nation in Africa nearing 200 million! Benedict was very adamant that Lagos would be the best city to be the pillar church for the continent of Africa! After a few days of prayer, Kip and Andrew agreed being persuaded by not only the population numbers, but also by knowledge that there were over 25 Nigerians in various SoldOut Movement Churches around the world that could move "home" to bolster the work. After that time, like the Man of Macedonia in Acts 16 who called Paul to come to the continent of Europe, Benedict has become known as the "Man of Nigeria!" Truly the Spirit has guided God's Movement as the Lagos International Christian Church was planted on June 26, 2016!

Benedict Atason was greeted by Jacque Groenewald,
Joel Parlor and Andrew Smellie when he arrived
at the First African Missions Conference!

As mentioned earlier, at the 2015 GLC, Elena received her
Doctorate Degree! Her dissertation was entitled, *ELEVATE
– Jesus' Global Revolution For Women!* After reading the
dissertation, Carlos and Lucy Mejia approached the
McKeans about publishing the dissertation as a book since
Hector Gomez of Bogota – the Editor of Berea Publishing
House – had recently joined the New Movement. In time,
Carlos asked Kip and the World Sector Leaders if he could
form a publishing house specifically to edit and print books
written by brothers and sisters in the SoldOut Movement.
This proposal was quickly accepted. Carlos became
President of SoldOut Press International. Since the first few
books that were published needed to be of the highest quality
of content and grammar, it was decided that Kip would
become Editor-in-Chief. He asked Lucy to be his Associate
Editor for English and Hector Gomez to be the Associate
Editor for the Spanish translations.

# SoldOut Press
## INTERNATIONAL

The Spanish galleon was selected for The SoldOut Press
International logo, because these glorious ships
sailed from Mexico bringing good news
back to the Old World!

At the 2016 GLC – **REVOLUTION,** Elena's dissertation
*ELEVATE* became available as a book in both English and
Spanish! As well, Andrew Smellie earned his ICCM
Doctorate Degree! Kip's vision was and is for all ICCM
Doctoral Dissertations to be published as books by SoldOut
Press International!

The beautiful cover photo for Elena's book *ELEVATE*
was taken by Mike Purdy!

Everyone was so excited for Elena to sign their copies of
*ELEVATE* everywhere Kip and Elena travelled!

*Eleve-se*
*Conferência de Mulheres 2017*

*"Ele declarou que lhes dará uma posição de glória, fama e honra muito acima de todas as nações que ele fez..." Deuteronômio 26:19*

*ELEVATE* has been an inspirational theme for
Women's Days around the world!

The Year of Family truly ended in glory! From a worldly
perspective, those of us who were close to the Paris Church
Leaders – Philippe and Prisca Scheidecker – were saddened
by the news that Prisca's cancer had returned for a third time.
The Lord blessed her with several more months of fruitful
labor. In fact, just two days before she passed on to glory on
December 22, 2016, Prisca led the Paris Women's Midweek!
A few weeks later at the 2017 Winter Workshop in Los
Angeles, there was a special half an hour dedicated to Prisca.

175

The McKeans and Philippe shared in tears about our dear sister Prisca. I will never forget Philippe's statement, "I did my job as Prisca's husband and got her to Heaven." Following the sharing a very moving tribute video was shown.

Philippe and Prisca Scheidecker baptized their daughter Rébecca in the Pacific Ocean on August 15, 2015 after the GLC!

This amazing Tribute Video dedicated to the memory of Prisca moved the thousands who viewed it at the 2017 Winter Workshop and on Facebook!

# 2017 THE YEAR OF
# THE IMPOSSIBLE

Inspirationally, 2017 for the SoldOut Movement was the Year of the Impossible! The impossible immediately began to happen in January as John Causey – once a vociferous opponent of the SoldOut Movement – called Kip seeking reconciliation. After spending several days studying, the Scriptures with Kip and Elena, John and Emma Causey joined God's New Movement on April 9, 2017! To introduce John to the Movement, in the *CAICC Bulletin* that John wrote to share how God led him to join the Movement, Kip wrote:

*First and foremost, I hold John Causey to be a very dear brother and friend. So, it gives me unfathomable joy to share with you that John and Emma Causey officially placed membership in the City of Angels ICC on April 9, 2017, thus joining God's new SoldOut Movement! John was baptized in 1979, as the first baptism of the Indiana State Campus Ministry. Emma was baptized through the efforts of the same Campus Ministry in 1982. They married in 1984. In 1989, the Causeys heard the call of God and entered the full-time ministry. During the 1990's, God used the Causeys to powerfully lead the Chicago Church, the London Church and the Metro Region of the LA ICOC, which we call the Southland Region.*

*After the ICOC's return to Mainline Church of Christ theology in 2002 and the ensuing falling away of thousands after the Kriete Letter in 2003, John became very involved in HOPEworldwide as a spokesman and a board member. In 2010, John was elected a founding member of the ICOC's Service Team of Eight who worked in collaboration to oversee what remained of the ICOC even though these congregations embraced autonomy. (The Service Team does not have a set leader.) Of note,*

*John was re-elected to the Service Team every year until his resignation last Fall. Also, John was the Coordinator for the LA ICOC Staff Meetings. In addition to these charges, John discipled the Church Leaders of the ICOC's Asia Pacific and Oceania Regions, who have a collective membership of over 10,000. With all of these responsibilities, John was arguably the most influential Evangelist in the ICOC until his self-imposed sabbatical and resignation from all responsibilities in October 2016. During these years, our beloved sister Emma developed a dynamic leadership training program for mothers and daughters called "Fine Pearls for Divine Girls." Please read John's remarkable account of how the Spirit led the Causeys into God's SoldOut Movement – in this our Year of the Impossible!*

On April 9, 2017, the impossible happened: John and Emma Causey placed membership in the City of Angels Church thus joining the SoldOut Movement!

Following Kip's introduction, John wrote the article for the *April 2017 CAICC Bulletin*. He entitled it, *Remember Those Earlier Days* in the spirit of Hebrews 10:32-39, **"Remember those earlier days after you received the light, when you**

178

*stood your ground in a great contest in the face of suffering... But we are not of those who shrink back and are destroyed, but of those who believe and are saved."*

This excerpt begins after John explained his personal background and the events that led to his baptism as a student at Indiana State University:

*...Scores of other students were baptized during my remaining three years. Also, my Mom, several family members, and the love of my life, Emma Jackson, became disciples! We were totally devoted to God's Word, to one-on-one discipling relationships, and to preaching the Word daily to our fellow students, friends and families. In 1982, our Campus Ministry started attending the new Boston World Missions Seminars, thus joining with Kip McKean and the Boston Total Commitment Movement to evangelize the nations.*

*Following graduation and two years of pure dating, [in 1984] Emma and I married and began an adventure beyond anything we could have "asked or imagined!" (Ephesians 3:20-21) ...*

*In 1999, we were called to lead the Metro Region of the LA ICOC and received discipling from Kip and Elena. Hundreds of souls were saved as God increased our numbers from 350 to almost 1,000! I still fondly remember July 2001, when God blessed our region to baptize over 100 people in one month! These were fruitful years! Emma and I fully embraced discipleship, our Movement's central leadership, Kip McKean as God's leader of our Movement, and the dream of the evangelization of the nations in this generation.*

*The year 2003 would begin a time of great challenge. During this year, two months after the Kriete Letter, the McKeans were unjustly fired as the LA ICOC Leaders and of the entire ICOC. It was then that our LA Region Leaders Group decided that we would no longer have a*

*"Lead" or "Senior" Evangelist to replace Kip's role in the LA Church. In retrospect, I now understand that we sinfully decided that each region should have "local independence" (autonomy), and that each region would operate and function locally – with no oversight or accountability from a central leadership. As a group, we did acknowledge that we should cooperate and function as eight equal parts of the larger LA Church. We selected a "Congregational Evangelist" – not the same as Lead Evangelist, as the Congregational Evangelist had no authority. He would only coordinate our agreed upon church-wide activities and had no discipleship or leadership oversight within the group. However, this decision for local autonomy and no formal group discipleship structure later led to the breakdown of discipleship throughout the entire church. What Kip has taught for now almost 40 years is true: "Autonomous churches beget autonomous disciples." The sin of autonomy isolates disciples, which allows Satan – the lion – to devour them. (1 Peter 5:8-9)*

*I personally want to take responsibility for my role in creating this independent and autonomous cloud within the LA ICOC. I deeply regret my influence in creating the unbiblical concept of a non-authoritative "Congregational Evangelist." Today, I sincerely apologize to the members of the LA ICOC, as I believe many members and leaders have been adversely affected by this decision to move away from the life-changing, healthy discipling relationships that we all need in our daily lives.*

*During the years of 2004 and 2005, I maintained contact with the McKeans when God moved them to Portland, Oregon. I attended the first two Portland Jubilees and observed Kip's leadership and continued commitment to church discipleship, central church leadership, and a visionary mission to reach all nations with the Gospel in our generation. However, in the Fall of 2005, I silently*

180

pulled back from the McKeans. With expressed reluctance – but to my eternal shame – I signed two letters sinfully disfellowshipping Kip from our churches. Sadly, for 12 years I had not followed up, sought any contact, or pursued reconciliation with a brother who had meant so much, and done so much in my spiritual life over the years! The Scriptures teach, *"Though a righteous man may fall seven times, seven times he gets back up!"* (Proverbs 24:16) God help us all, if in sinful judgment, we believe any disciple cannot get back up!

From 2015 to 2016, God began a period of discipline and refinement in my spiritual life. During this period, I travelled in excess of 200,000 miles around the world: Multiple trips to Asia, Europe, Africa and the Pacific Islands, as well as several US domestic trips serving the ICOC Churches and HOPEworldwide. In June of 2016, I realized I had become very emotionally and spiritually tired from trying to help – but with little success – with the many serious challenges inside HOPEworldwide and our struggling churches. Gordon Ferguson – an ICOC Elder and an outspoken opponent of the SoldOut Movement – stated what I sensed from my travels to be true in his book *My Three Lives – The Story Of One Man And Three Movements*:

> The ICOC [in 2015 had] 667 congregations overall. 381 baptized one to 10 people and 122 had zero baptisms. Thus, in our 667 churches, 503 (75%) baptized between zero and 10 people. And let me state the obvious here – when baptisms are so few – things are not close to going well.

I discussed my exhaustion with my local staff, requesting some time off to recover spiritually. The staff was supportive, yet others would not act upon or honor this request. I tried to soldier on, only to realize I was more than weary; I was completely burnt out. For me it would

181

*require significant time away from ministry in order to spend time with God to revive and refresh my soul.*

*So, in October 2016, I resigned from my role as the Metro Region Leader of the LA ICOC. I resigned from the ICOC Service Team. I removed myself from oversight and partnership roles with the churches in Oceania, Asia and in particular the Philippines. For the next five months, I devoted myself to prayer, fasting, Bible study and wrestling with God, to gain clarity and understanding of my spiritual condition and His future will for my life. This began a time of intense spiritual revelation, pain, loneliness, streams of tears, cries for God's mercy, and a plea for the Holy Spirit to fill up my empty heart and life! Today I thank God for this time of suffering. He has filled my heart with fire again, refreshed my soul, and caused me to remember the core convictions of my conversion to Christ! During this time, Psalms 25 and 86 provided such a guiding light.*

*In the fall of 2016, I wrestled with the question, "Why are the ICOC Churches not growing but instead filled with seemingly unresolvable issues that wore me out?" After studying the Word, I came to a deep conviction that central leadership is God's plan to lead His people, so they will not become* **"sheep without a shepherd."** *(Numbers 27:15-18) After abandoning our father in the faith Kip, we became a group of churches led by the ears and not visionary eyes. So, in January 2017, following another Bible study on reconciliation, God put it on my heart to reach out to Kip. I realized after all that happened in 2003, it had now been 14 years! 14 years ago! I immediately reached out by phone and, in tears, apologized for my blindness of all that God was doing in the SoldOut Movement, for being a part of all the judgment, for allowing years to pass, for the hurt and pain that he and Elena had experienced by shaming them through a false disfellowshipment. Kip responded with warmth, openness and forgiveness. He expressed with*

182

*humility all that God had put him through. Kip shared with me the lessons he needed to learn about humility, forgiveness, reliance on God, and having mercy for the weak.*

*Early last month in March 2017, Emma and I were invited to dinner by Kip and Elena at their home. Following this incredible reunion, I was refreshed and greatly encouraged by two days of discussions with Kip about his life, convictions and lessons learned from God. I will never forget the time that Kip and I walked up Mt. Hollywood (which he affectionately calls Mt. Shalom), got down on our knees crying together and prayed about our lives, our families, the city of LA, and the nations of the world! Though I found Kip to be a confident leader, I clearly saw how God had transformed Kip's natural confidence to be a confidence in God alone. I was very encouraged to see the mercy, grace and love that Kip has for all the brothers and sisters in the ICOC, in spite of the hurt and separation that Kip and his family had experienced. I expressed to Kip that I was proud of his relationship with God and his inspiring transformation. I let him know that, "My happiest and most fruitful times were serving under his leadership" and that "as it was in the earlier days, he remains a visionary leader and God's man in this generation!"*

*The next day, I visited the LA Staff Meeting of the International Christian Churches. I was blown away by what my eyes saw! I witnessed fire in the singing, zeal while sharing about the previous week's baptisms, and an incredible warmth in the fellowship... then I **"remembered those earlier days after [I] received the light"** as a college student in God's Movement! This was the church that I was baptized in! I was so inspired by the excitement of the mature disciples, and scores of young 19 to 23-year olds, who were passionate to be full-time in the ministry! I was very convicted that my own judgmental heart and lack of faith did not allow me to see how the*

*Spirit was moving in the New Movement. After a long fellowship, I left and prayed most of that day, thanking God for what my eyes and heart had just seen. (Luke 10:23-24) I was reminded that day, that there is a huge difference between a group of churches that form a fellowship and the Movement of God!*

*On another occasion, I apologized to my friend Kip that I was the one who sent Evangelists and Elders to Hilo, Hawaii in September 2006 to oppose Kip and Elena's efforts to help the young ministry leaders – Kyle and Joan Bartholomew – revive the Hilo Church. Ironically, I have come to understand that this singular action caused Kip and the Portland Leaders to conclude that God was saying to them that there was **"no remedy"** (2 Chronicles 36:15-16) to cure the ICOC. Thus, from this incident, the Spirit sparked the New Movement – the International Christian Churches (ICC)! Today, I clearly see that the New Movement is "THE Movement of God" and Kip is God's man for this generation – and always has been!*

*Today, I am very thankful for this journey. I have made many mistakes and fallen down many times. Yet God has graciously raised me to my feet again! I am looking forward to this next chapter in my spiritual journey with God and His Movement... Clearly this is not a movement of men, but THE very Movement of God! To God be all the glory!*

Another of the many highlights of the Year of the Impossible was the explosive growth by the Dubai International Christian Church! Since RD Baker had planted the Bahrain ICOC in the 90's, Kip asked RD and his wife April to lead the Dubai Mission Team. Kip was led to believe that this would be a difficult decision for them as April has a very serious heart defect. Upon their wholehearted acceptance of this call by the Spirit in January 2016, April's heart was functioning at 40%. RD and April received strong persecution from April's family, who had fallen away from the Lord. They could not comprehend why the Bakers would leave the excellent and free health care offered since birth by UCLA. On Sunday, August 21, 2016 the Eleventh Crown of Thorns Mission Team – Dubai – was sent off from the Chicago Church! Incredibly, inspired by her daughter's zeal to die doing something significant for God, April's mother Robin Diaz was restored in the City of Angels Church that very Sunday!

RD and April Baker received the customary specialty cake given to the Mission Team Leaders at their last City of Angels Staff Meeting before they left for the mission field!

On Friday, September 23, 2016 was the Inaugural Service of the Dubai ICC! With just nine on the mission team and only the McKeans as visiting disciples, God blessed them with an amazing 56 in attendance! That Fall, there were six restorations and place memberships directly from our former fellowship. However, there were no baptisms. Therefore, in mid-January the McKeans flew to Dubai to encourage the church. Of the mission team of nine, three had to return to their home nations in late December. Sensing a need to strengthen the Dubai Church, the McKeans brought RJ Castro who had been on the Manila Mission Team and had built the Rizal Technical University Campus Ministry from one to 25 in the last six months of his time in Manila.

In April, the Bakers returned to LA for April's tri-annual check-up with her cardiologist. Upon their return, there was an unknown reason for the immense swelling in one of her knees. While she was in the hospital for treatment on her knee, April suffered a heart attack that led to a complete cardiac arrest. By the providence of God, RD was at her side when this occurred! He immediately started yelling for help! When the first nurse arrived, she began CPR. RD was ushered out of the room as a team of now 15 doctors and nurses gathered around April. For four long minutes April's heart did not beat, and being in anguish, RD prayed to the Lord to spare April's life. "Impossibly," she was brought back to life and RD overheard a doctor say, "If I believed in God, I would say this young woman received God's grace!" Though April's heart after the cardiac arrest plunged to just 20% functionality, through prayer and juicing (a form of fasting encouraged by the McKeans), by mid-July her heart had recovered to 40% again! Her cardiologist – who was against her going to Dubai initially – gave his approval for her to return!

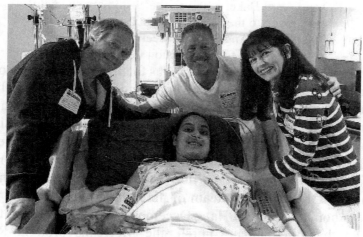

April was surprisingly vibrant just hours after her cardiac arrest!

RD and April returned to Dubai in late July and then flew on to Manila for the 2017 GLC where April was appointed a Women's Ministry Leader! Astonishingly, there at the GLC, the Bakers reported that in the first 28 weeks of the year, the Dubai Church has miraculously grown by 23 additions – 21 baptisms, 1 restoration and 1 place membership and only one fall away! And to God be all the glory!

The incredible Dubai ICC on May 27, 2017!

In this Year of the Impossible, another light that continued to burn brighter and brighter – the International College of Christian Ministries! Kip spent four years personally developing the curriculum for the ICCM's Bachelor's, Master's and Doctorate Degrees. It was exciting for all of us in the SoldOut Movement to see Kip's vision become reality in the proliferation of the ICCM to other cities! As mentioned before, a lead Evangelist with an ICCM Master's Degree has the privilege of opening an ICCM extension campus. As of August 2017, there were extension campuses in Boston, Lagos, Manila, Portland, São Paulo, Toronto and Washington DC! I was privileged to be the IT Registrar for ICCM-Global. My first assignment was to develop ID Cards for every ICCM Student around the world!

The ICCM ID Cards were designed by the author!

The ICCM-Global Faculty and Extension Campus
Presidents and Deans of Women
in August 2016!

Kip taught The Ten Commandments Of Preaching for the
2016 September Session of the ICCM-Manila!

At the beginning of 2017, Kip laid out before the Lord and
the Movement a plan to have discipling ministries in every
state in America! He called this OPERATION EAGLE. (The
eagle is America's national bird.) It was a simple plan. In
2018 in the SoldOut Movement, planned were two church
plantings in the United States in states that did not have a
SoldOut Congregation; in 2019 there would be three
plantings; in 2020 four plantings; in 2021 five plantings; in
2022 six plantings; in 2023 seven plantings; and in 2024
there would be eight plantings in the America and thus all 50
States would have SoldOut Movement Churches!

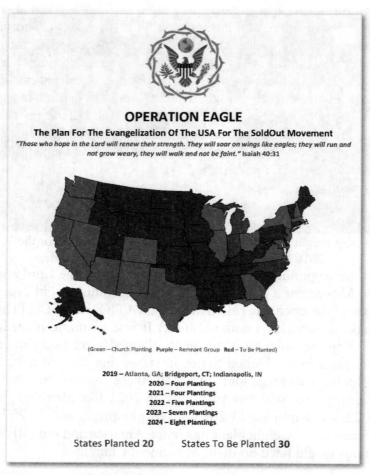

## OPERATION EAGLE

**The Plan For The Evangelization Of The USA For The SoldOut Movement**

*"Those who hope in the Lord will renew their strength. They will soar on wings like eagles; they will run and not grow weary, they will walk and not be faint."* Isaiah 40:31

(Green – Church Planting  Purple – Remnant Group  Red – To Be Planted)

**2019** – Atlanta, GA; Bridgeport, CT; Indianapolis, IN
**2020** – Four Plantings
**2021** – Four Plantings
**2022** – Five Plantings
**2023** – Seven Plantings
**2024** – Eight Plantings

States Planted **20**        States To Be Planted **30**

The OPERATION EAGLE Project
as of February 2019!

This extraordinary plan excited the disciples in America, as most disciples' families would be much closer to a discipling church enhancing the hope of their conversion. It excited particularly the church leaders of the international churches, as more American Churches meant that God would provide more money for missions!

Perhaps, the most exciting event in 2017 was the planting of our Twelfth and final Crown of Thorns Church – Hong Kong, China! Hong Kong is a city with a population of 7.5

million and is the gateway to the 1.4 billion lost souls of China! The goal of Phase One of the Crown of Thorns Project was to place churches in arguably the 12 most influential cities of the world (guided by remnant groups), as these cities influence not only their nation but the nations in their surrounding region. Collectively, all 196 nations in the world are influenced by the United States and the Crown of Thorns Cities! Very interestingly, the Sydney Church converted so many Chinese Nationals that was the sending church for the Hong Kong Planting. With Kip's call for nationals to go home to evangelize their nations, Chi Leong – who was converted in Chicago – moved to Sydney to train to lead the Hong Kong Mission Team. Chi supported himself to be trained full-time with his lifetime savings of $26,000!

The 2017 GLC – VICTORIOUS – was the first GLC held outside of the United States! Selected for the honor of hosting was the Metro Manila ICC! Highlights included the memorable Kingdom Appointments of Chi Leong – the Hong Kong, Mission Team Leader – and Aaron & Sharmayne Viscichini then of New York City. Also, there was the extraordinary Fifth Commencement of the International College of Christian Ministries where 93 degrees were conferred. I will not soon forget that upon the hooding of Raul Felipe Moreno to receive his well-earned Doctorate Degree, the crowd stood on their feet and gave a thunderous applause of appreciation! Ensuing was the exhilarating Send-Offs of the Cebu, Guam, Miami/Ft. Lauderdale and the Twelfth (and last) Crown of Thorns Mission Team – Hong Kong!

191

The fired up Hong Kong Mission Team at
their 2017 GLC Send-Off!

Tim Kernan's book 20/20 shared
the gleanings of Kip's
LA Staff Meetings!

Though 2017 was more than fulfilling its theme as the Year
of the Impossible, Kip sensed in mid-June ever-increasing
attacks on God's Movement by Satan and his demons! It was

192

at this time that Elena bought the movie *War Room* for them to watch. The movie inspired Kip to set up a **Prayer War Room** at the 2017 GLC remembering Revelation 12:7, 17, *"And there was war in Heaven... But the great dragon [Satan] was hurled to the earth, and his angels with him... Then the dragon was enraged. and went off to make war against... those who obey God's commandments and hold to the testimony of Jesus."* This Scripture clearly teaches that Satan is at war with every disciple! The Prayer War Room opened at 5:00PM on Tuesday of the GLC. For the duration of the conference, at least one disciple prayed on their knees each hour – day and night – for the remaining six days of the GLC! As well, "sticky notes" (post-its) and pens were provided so that each disciple could write down their prayer requests and place them on the walls for those who would follow, so they could pray for each other's prayers.

Karen Maciel – Kip's and Elena's trusted assistant – opened up the Prayer War Room at 5PM on Tuesday, August 1st!

The inspired Prayer War Room on Sunday, August 6th!!

After the conclusion of the early Saturday morning MERCY Rally at 8:00AM, the GLC international delegates boarded 60 jeepneys – small local buses! With a very formidable police escort, it took about an hour to travel from our hotel in Makati to Mandaluyong!

The MERCY Event received an impressive Police Escort!

The actual site of the GLC MERCY Event was in a very poor section of Mandaluyong called Welfareville at the Jose

Fabella Memorial School! Interestingly, the city motto for Mandaluyong – also called Tiger City – is in Tagalog "Gawa Hindi Salita" – "Act Not Talk!" This is exactly what we did! From 7:00AM to 9:00AM a group of Filipino and disciple doctors, dentists and nurses examined the 300 children of "squatters" that were asked to participate in the MERCY Event! (A "squatter" is an individual that moved from the province to the city to better his family's life. Often this family lived in a small area – maybe 10 feet by 10 feet – and there built a tin, plywood or sometimes cardboard home. Most individuals in Welfareville make a salary of $2-3 per day.)

The children received free medical and dental care!
Upon arriving near the Jose Fabella Memorial School, the streets were lined with thousands of cheering local residents and school children as the community was so excited that a "Christian Group" made up of members from nations across the globe were coming to serve them! The 300 Filipino children sat at their desks and almost 1,000 MERCY Ambassadors (240 Filipino and 650 international) paid individual attention to them!

Kip and the author's son Dylan shared a special moment with a grateful child!

To begin the MERCY Event Program, selected children sang songs to us as a choir! Lauren Ona-Zepeda – our dear LA sister – mesmerized her fellow Filipinos in the crowd with her singing! Following, the Honorable Carmelita "Menchie" Abalos – the first woman Mayor of Mandaluyong City – was presented with the crystal Global Ambassador Award by Nick and Denise Bordieri! Then, Mayor Abalos gave a short speech of appreciation for *MERCYworldwide* and for the International Christian Churches! Upon concluding her remarks, she graciously presented Kip & Elena with a key to Mandaluyong City!

Elena was greeted by the Mayor of Mandaluyong City –
the Honorable Carmelita "Menchie" Abalos!

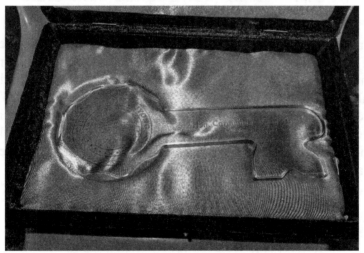

The key to Mandaluyong City was presented by
Mayor Abalos to the McKeans!

Then the children received more food to take home to their
families, as well as "MERCY backpacks" with school
supplies – given to them through the sacrifice of the Sydney
Disciples! By 1:30PM, the children and all of us were
thoroughly exhausted from the event and the sweltering

heat! Taking jeepneys once again, we arrived back at the hotel around 2:30PM.

The unforgettable Closing Ceremony of the
2017 Day of MERCY!

On Sunday, placing membership were Blady & Cielo Perez of Phnom Penh, Cambodia – who up to that moment were paid by the ICOC! As is our custom, if someone is presently full-time in the ICOC and hears the Spirit's call into God's New Movement, we will offer them a full-time position in the International Christian Churches! So, with Blady, Cielo and their son Bryce placing membership, instantly created was the Phnom Penh ICC Remnant Group!

When Blady and Cielo Perez took their stand against the
ICOC's false doctrines and lukewarmness, they
initiated the Phnom Penh Remnant Group!

On Thursday, August 10th, our sister AJ Castillo – who
reported directly to President Duterte – escorted the
Untalans, the Bordieris, the Carbonells, the Kernans, Ronnie
Gonzalez, and the McKeans to possibly meet President
Duterte at the Malacañan Palace! Upon arrival, they were
informed that President Duterte had flown back to his home
city of Davao for an emergency. However, President Duterte
had the number two man in the Philippine Government –
Secretary Ernesto Abella – greet the group! They spent a
good half an hour with him sharing about MERCY, the
International Christian Churches, and since he had already
read about the MERCY Event in Welfareville in the
newspaper, they talked about that the most! Of course, Kip
invited him to church and he seemed interested! He privately
shared with AJ and Kip that Kip would most likely have the
chance to present to President Duterte the Bible that Kip had
inscribed for him when Kip returned to Manila! Please be
praying for this opportunity so that like Paul, we can preach
to the *"Gentiles and their kings!"* (Acts 9:15)

Kip presented Secretary Abella with a gift
for President Duterte!!

Praise God that in 2017, there were new discipling churches planted in Birmingham, England; Kona, Hawaii; Monterrey, Mexico; Rio de Janeiro, Brazil; Kiev, Ukraine; Guam; Cebu, Philippines; Miami/Ft. Lauderdale; and the Twelfth Crown of Thorns Church – Hong Kong, China! So, God has added nine church plantings in 2017 – the most ever for our Movement in a single year!

History was made on September 3, 2017 as the Twelfth and final Crown of Thorns Church – Hong Kong – celebrated their Inaugural Service! With the eminent threat of Typhoon Mawar forecasted three days before to hit Hong Kong that weekend, many would have been disheartened. However, the Hong Kong Mission Team – trained in the radical Sydney Church by Joe & Kerry Willis – preached the Word every day that whole week believing that the God of Elijah was with them! *"Elijah was a man just like us. He prayed earnestly that it would not rain and it did not rain on the land for three and a half years!"* (James 5:17) God answered this "impossible prayer" and so with no rain that afternoon, they met at 4:00PM on the 17th floor of one of the many high rises in that great metropolis!

The remarkable "Hong Kong Seven" on the mission team – and Joe & Kerry Willis and Kip as the only supporting disciples – were blessed by God with an extraordinary attendance of exactly 35! There were no children as almost all the visitors were very open college students from the Polytechnic University of Hong Kong! In fact, decided was to conduct this service and future ones in English!

On November 18, 2017, Kip's beloved father Admiral Thomas W. McKean unexpectantly passed away at 89 years old. At the Memorial Service, the following Saturday, over 25 of his closest friends in the Movement flew to Orlando from all around the world to be by his side at this dark hour.

A touching tribute to his father written by Kip and was passed out to all who attended the memorial service!

Not only did Kip preach a moving message at the service but he wrote, *Rear Admiral Thomas McKean – A Tribute of Admiration and Affection:*

*"Fair Winds and Following Seas" is a toast or salutation between mariners. It implies that a ship will have favorable winds and not have to pound into the waves, for*

*on a perfect sailing day, the wind direction is the same as the waves. Such was the life of my father – Rear Admiral Thomas Wayne McKean, USN (Retired). A dear neighbor wrote to my mother this week, "Tom was a great man of so much knowledge and character." Dad was born to Dr. Gorman F. McKean and Elmira (Stanley) McKean on May 18, 1928 in Adams County, Indiana. He lived his younger years until college in the small farming community of 1,800 in Montpelier, Indiana. In high school, Dad excelled in athletics as he earned three letters in basketball, three in track, and four in baseball, as well as played saxophone in the band. However, to do well in academics, it was not always "smooth sailing" as Dad had to make the extra effort to do well.*

*In 1946 – a year after World War II ended – Dad graduated high school and headed to Indiana University. In God's sovereignty on the first day of Dad's freshman English Class, he met his future wife – my Mom – Marilyn Ruth "Kim" Kimberlin. He also pledged Sigma Chi Fraternity where decades later he was recognized as a "Significant Sig". Inspired, I too pledged Sigma Chi as a freshman some 25 years later.*

*During his college years, Dad developed a desire to go into the Navy, so he joined ROTC. Following in the steps of his father who was a dentist, Dad was accepted into Indiana University Dental School in 1949 and was awarded a full Navy scholarship. In 1952 on August 9th, Dad married the love of his life – Mom! Upon graduation in 1953, he was commissioned a Lieutenant JG.*

*I was his first child born on May 31, 1954 and named Thomas Wayne II. He did not "meet me" until six months later as he was "at sea" serving with the Marines in the Sahara Desert alongside the French Foreign Legion. To complete his sea duty, although tough on Mom, they left for four months to the Caribbean where he was involved in the movie Away All Boats starring Jeff Chandler. My*

202

awesome brother "Randall" was named for Dad's first ship the USS Randall APA 224. "Randy" was born on February 29, 1956 during Dad's tour at the Naval Academy. Eight years later while serving at the Boston Naval Shipyard, his precious daughter Dana was born on May 3, 1964.

After completing his residency in Oral Surgery at Great Lakes Naval Training Center in 1965, Dad had the great honor to be stationed on the then newest aircraft carrier in the Navy, the USS America CVA 66. While serving on the USS America during the Vietnam War, Dad performed surgery on hundreds of critically wounded soldiers. After two years, our family was elated that Dad passed the Maxillofacial Surgery Boards and was promoted to Captain.

A year or so later, it was as the Commander of the Naval Hospitals of the Southern United States that Dad encountered the rough seas of prejudice and chauvinism in the Navy. Yet it was then that Dad further distinguished himself. Courageously risking his future advancement in rank by taking a stand for civil rights and women's rights, Dad relieved senior officers (not in authority but in years to him) of their commands when he found miscarriages of justice and equality. Later because of his optimistic perseverance, Dad was given two bronze irons as bookends, because he always exhorted those under his charge – no matter the cost or the challenges – "Press on!"

In 1980, I still remember Dad phoning me and enthusiastically sharing about the call he just received from the Surgeon General congratulating him on being selected to be one of only four Admirals in the US Naval Dental Corps. Though Dad was controversial for his convictions, Admiral George Besbekos was instrumental in Dad being selected as the first Oral Surgeon Admiral in the history of the Navy. In 1982, Dad was promoted to

*RADM – UH (upper-half) and became the first dentist to hold the illustrious office of Inspector General for the Medical/Dental Department of the Navy. Again historic, for most have a higher regard for "life-saving doctors" over "mere dentists" Of course, Dad was a Maxillofacial surgeon that did save many lives. With our incredible mother traveling with him, Dad literally inspected US Naval Hospitals around the world from London to Cairo to Manila in his final post for three years. Dad retired on October 1, 1985 at only 57 years old after 36 years in the Navy.*

*Ever active, Dad became Chairman of the Florida Hospital Foundation Board in 1994. He later served for 16 years as a Founder and Chairman of Florida Shares of the Florida Hospital Foundation of International Medical Missions. I was very moved that in Dad's retirement years, his faith in Christ and in the power of prayer significantly grew through the "Healing Ministries" and the First United Methodist Church of Winter Park. One of Dad's favorite Scriptures was, "The prayer of a righteous man is powerful and effective. Elijah was a man just like us. He prayed earnestly that it would not rain, and it did not rain on the land for three and a half years." (James 5:16-17) Dad humbly believed that his prayers – as well as countless others – cured Randy of cancer as a teen, restored me to health from boils in my college years, and healed Elena of bone cancer three years ago.*

*Dad also was very involved in his beloved Village on the Green in Longwood, Florida, where Dad and Mom have lived for over six years, and where Dad's parents – Grampy and Grammy – spent their final happy years. Dad has spent his energies to improve this amazing place, especially advocating for the expansion of the Health Center. Earlier this year, Dad – forever a patriot – addressed the residents of Village on the Green concluding with the stirring words, "Remember that it is the veteran who has given us freedom of religion, freedom to assemble, the right to a fair trial, the right to vote, and the honor to salute the flag. God Bless America!" The final highlight of Dad's life was just three months ago on August 9th, as Dad and Mom celebrated their 65th Wedding Anniversary. Dad passed away at age 89 on Saturday morning, November 18, 2017 at the Village on the Green. As Dad would have it, he passed quietly while sitting on a bench after winning his final Bocce Ball Match.*

*Dad was the adored patriarch of the McKean Family. His legacy of fighting for and expecting moral excellence remains through his best friend – Mom, their three children, seven grandchildren, and ten great-grandchildren. Dad was my first hero and has been and forever will be a guiding light. I am confident that his charge and prayer for all of us would simply be, "Press on and MAKE 'Fair Winds and Following Seas!'"*

RADM Thomas Wayne McKean (1928 – 2017)

So the Year of the Impossible closed in sadness, as all of us in the Movement felt Kip's pain at the loss of his father. Indeed, death is "impossible" to escape, so this is why we strive for the evangelization of the nations in this generation! After a time of mourning, Kip's spirits were lifted as he dutifully prepared himself through prayer and fasting for 2018 – the Year of Grace!

From all over the world, 25 of Kip's closest friends flew to be
by his side to mourn the passing of his father.

# 2018 THE YEAR OF GRACE

The Year of Grace may well be remembered for so many weddings including: Tulio & Vaitsa Amaral, Caio & Carol Costa and Vini & Bia Rodriguez all of Brazil, and of course, the new AMS Global Leaders – Adam & Lauren Zepeda!

Kip's keynote lesson at the 2018 LAMC was was Conviction of the Heart!

The Year of Grace was highlighted by so many miracles not the least of which are the three OPERATION Eagle plantings: Albuquerque, New Mexico; Milwaukee, Wisconsin; and the 19th OPERATION Eagle Church – Columbus, Ohio! In total, a record 10 churches were planted around the world! Internationally, of note there was the Kinshasa (Democratic Republic of Congo) Church Reconstruction where there are now 308 disciples!

The other standout international planting was New Delhi, India! Raja Rajan – the New Delhi Mission Team Leader – reported in late November:

*Greetings from the capital city of India's 1.3 billion people! God has been gracious to the New Delhi Mission Team known as the "Spartans!" The 38-member mission team landed on April 28, 2018. The next day was our very first Sunday and God blessed us with 205 in attendance! In seven months, we have seen 93 miracles – 70 baptisms, 22 restorations and 1 place membership! Our Teen Ministry, which started with only our daughter Isheeta, now has grown to 31 teens! We now have 138 New Delhi Disciples! At our recent All India Leadership Retreat, affirmed, but still God willing, is that the mission teams to Kathmandu (Nepal), and Kolkata (India) will be sent out during the South Asia Mission Conference in November 2019!*

The Powerful New Dehli Mission Team was
nicknamed the Spartans!

Another exciting **"evidence of the grace of God… [as] a great number of people were brought to the Lord"** on the Isle of Hispaniola in the Caribbean! (Acts 11:23-24) Hispaniola has the nation of Haiti on the westside and the Dominican Republic on the eastside. According to the *CIA World Factbook*, Haiti is recognized as the poorest country in the Western Hemisphere. In January 2010, Haiti experienced a devastating 7.0 earthquake in which about 300,000 people died and 1.5 million were left homeless! The country has yet to fully recover from that catastrophe!

In 2013, Alexis Turgeau – a Haitian Church of Christ preacher in Port-au-Prince – contacted Kip seeking spiritual revival for himself and for his beloved nation. Kip "tested Alexis' sincerity" by inviting him to the 2013 Global Leadership Conference (GLC), while not offering any financial assistance. After studying the First Principles with our French-speaking Evangelists – Tim Kernan, Amadou Sountoura and Blaise Feumba – during the GLC, Alexis was baptized as a sold-out disciple!

Alexis Turgeau – a former Church of Christ minister – studied the Bible and was the first baptism of all the SoldOut Movement Haitian Churches!

Alexis left LA resolved and eager to take the radical message of Christ to his family, friends and fellow Churches of Christ preachers in Haiti! In September 2013, Kip sent Blaise to travel to Port-au-Prince, the capital city of Haiti, to study with Alexis' family and friends. During that missionary journey, seven Church of Christ preachers repented and were baptized as "true disciples" of Jesus Christ! By October 2018, Blaise shared that after five years and five additional missionary trips later, and after a total of 19 Church of Christ preachers were baptized as disciples, the Movement had 10 Haitian Churches with the total of almost 400 disciples!

On Blaise's 2018 missionary journey, he travelled the dangerous roads from Haiti to go into the Dominican Republic. The two countries of Haiti and the Dominican Republic are not only linked by geography but by a common history, as they were both formed by African slaves and at one point were one country called Saint Domingue. After a nine-hour drive, Blaise and his band of brothers finally arrived in El Pocito, a small town in the north of the Dominican Republic.

They were warmly welcomed to El Pocito by Chelot & Amecia Francois – the lead couple of a Church of Christ of about 80 members. They were blown away by the church's hospitality, as we later learned that their poor congregation had been collecting money to build a bedroom extension in their venue to host Blaise and his fellow traveling evangelists. Some even sacrificed the equivalent of an entire month's wage to accomplish this goal! After preaching and teaching for five days, 23 were baptized! Thus, formed was the first SoldOut Movement Church in the Dominican Republic – the El Pocito ICC – led by the newly baptized Chelot and Amecia!

In August, the 2018 GLC was back in Los Angeles! Kip wrote in the *August 31st Good News Email:*

*Truly, the 2018 Global Leadership Conference –* **EMPOWERED** *– was our best one... yet! The Sunday Worship Service will surely be talked about in Heaven! The singing by the almost 2,700 in attendance was angelic! In the Communion, RD & April Baker – LA's new Ventura Region Leaders and heroes of the Middle East – brought us to the cross! Joe & Kerry Willis were hysterical in motivating us to give generously at the Contribution Charge! Then came the glorious Sixth GLC Commencement of the International College of Christian Ministries where a record 92 received their BA Degrees and a record six received the prestigious Master's Degree! Dr. Andrew Smellie of Lagos gave the message* *of the hour on Transforming Power! Following, we witnessed 21 souls make their "good confession" and then were baptized into Christ! After these amazing miracles, we prayed on our knees for the Holy Spirit to send out the Columbus (Ohio) and Milwaukee (Wisconsin) OPERATION Eagle Mission Teams, as well as to send out Nick & Denise Bordieri to Phnom Penh (Cambodia) to establish and oversee the Chhem MERCY Orphanage for the next year! To close the service, we stood arm-in-arm singing with LuJack Martinez The Glory Song – International Version! And to God was given all the glory!*

As the Editor for SoldOut Press International, Kip gave great emphasis at the 2018 GLC to the two new books from SoldOut Press: *A Battle That Even Kings Lost – Winning Your Battle For Sexual Purity* by Raul Moreno and *Money Is The Answer For Everything* by Joe Willis. At the GLC Church Builders Workshop, Kip called on the evangelists to prepare their congregations for the usual January pledge drive by purchasing Joe's book for every member and going through it together for their quiet times in December.

Ground-breaking books by Raul
Moreno and Joe Willis, inspired
the entire Movement!

Though there were many terrific speeches given at the 2018 GLC, the one that had the most impact was Kip's 90-minute presentation: A Greater Glory – The History of the Mainline Churches of Christ, the ICOC and the SoldOut Movement. Most Christians understand that for every event – whether good or bad – in their life there is at least one Scripture "parallel." Not considered by many Christians is that this same principle holds true for God's people, God's Movements.

Therefore, using the Books of 2 Chronicles, Ezra, Nehemiah and Haggai, Kip soberly led us in a study of the account that God decimated the beautiful Solomon's Temple, because there was *"no remedy"* to motivate the Jews to repent. So, God sent His people into exile in Babylon for 70 years, and then called them back to Jerusalem as a purified remnant to build the Second Temple. Though this Second Temple was quite modest as it was made of the charred stones from the First Temple, Haggai preached that, *"The glory of this present house will be greater than the glory of the former house"* (Haggai 2:9) Kip gave this account as a "parallel" to God's destruction of the ICOC, and His grace building the new SoldOut Movement!

Of the two most critical issues that Kip addressed, the first was, "What does it mean to evangelize the nations in a generation?" Kip stated that it is not that everyone in the world becomes a disciple or is studied with. Then he shared that the evangelization of the nations is not even the completion of the Crown of Thorns Project with a church in every nation! It simply means the same as it did in the first century description by Paul in Colossians 1:23, *"...This is the Gospel that you heard and that has been proclaimed to every creature under Heaven."* It merely means that everyone has heard of the true Gospel of Jesus! Astonishingly, most will hear through persecution. In underscoring what it means to evangelize the nations in this generation, Kip has preached on countless occasions, "Nike, McDonalds, Starbucks and Beyoncé have already evangelized the world in "this generation!" It does not mean that everyone wears Nikes, eats McDonald hamburgers, drinks Starbucks, or even likes to listen to Beyoncé. It simply means that everyone has heard!" We will evangelize the world when everyone has heard either by disciples' personal preachings or by public persecution in the media, which should happen long before the SoldOut Movement plants churches in all 196 nations.

The CyberMinistry, as of 2018 included the newly appointed CyberWML's – Alicia Dunn, Jacque Economo and Chantelle Anderson, will acceleralate the evangelation of the nations!

So important as well, Kip gave us a better understanding of a second issue: The rate of growth in the Boston Movement versus the SoldOut Movement. Most people parallel the beginning of the Boston Movement in 1979 to the beginning of the SoldOut Movement in 2007, and it does have some parallels such as the McKeans beginning to lead this effort. However, Kip explained that when it comes to growth, this not a "apples-to-apples comparison."

Since the Portland Church departed the Movement in 2008, essentially the seed for the entire New Movement was the 42 Portland Disciples on the City of Angels Missions Team. Having only one congregation to "start a movement" is best paralleled to the beginning of the Crossroads Movement, where there was only one Mainline Church. The SoldOut

Movement is 11 years old and has over 7,000 disciples in almost 100 churches in 38 countries. In the 11th year of the Crossroads Movement in 1979, there were no discipling ministries outside the USA and there were around 40 or so Campus Ministry / Crossroads Churches. We were encouraged to hear that we are "far ahead" numerically and geographically than the first 11 years of the Crossroads Movement.

As well, Kip reminded us that the Boston Church – among the Crossroads Ministries – was uniquely built where everyone in the church was totally committed. This made moving to the Boston Church to be very attractive for zealous college graduates seeking to do great things for God from the 40-some Crossroads Campus Ministry Churches, as well as from "other lower profile campus ministry movements" led by Milton Jones, John Wilson and Steve Eckstein. So, from the very beginning in 1979, there was a steady flow of dynamic college graduates moving to become members of the Boston Church and later her plantings as well.

Then from 1985 to 1987 (after Chuck Lucas left the ministry and the differences between the Boston Church and the Crossroads Ministries became very apparent), about 3,000 young and idealist remnant disciples came into the Boston Movement from the Crossroads Movement thus greatly accelerating the exponential growth in Boston! In the New Movement, Kip shared that the remnant has been far fewer, and that they for the most part are wounded, hurting and aging adults much like the Second Temple's charred stones – needing much attention.

So, the primary reasons for the difference in the growth rate between the Boston Movement and the SoldOut Movement can be summed up by: 1) The incredible differences in the two remnants with which God brought into the two movements – "young and zealous" versus "old and wounded." 2) The sheer numbers of the remnant who were

216

capable of leadership and being sent out – "thousands" versus "hundreds." Added to this, Kip and the Boston Leaders reconstructed the Crossroads Churches that wanted to join them into churches completely composed of "totally committed or sold-out disciples" through reconstructions, again adding thousands more available for forceful advancement. Therefore, the final charge from Kip to all of the SoldOut Movement Churches was to refocus our efforts on the campuses to produce by baptism (instead of through the remnant) the influx of thousands of zealous college students that will lead to the same exponential growth as seen in the Boston Movement.

One of the ultimate signs of grace in this Year of Grace was on Easter Sunday: Kyle Bartholomew's tearful restoration to the Lord and His people! Sadly, in mid-2017, Kyle and his wife Joan had both broke their marriage vows forcing Kip to remove them from the Metro Manila Church Leadership and to step them out of the full-time ministry immediately following the 2017 GLC. Kyle and Joan headed home from Manila to Hilo with their three children as Kyle had fallen away. Shortly afterward, sadder yet, Joan left Kyle and the children for months with no contact, as she too fell away.

At his restoration, Kyle shared Micah 7:8-9, *"Though I have fallen, I will rise. Though I sit in darkness, the Lord will be my light. Because I have sinned against Him, I will bear the Lord's wrath, until He pleads my case and establishes my right. He will bring me out into the light; I will see His righteousness."* Kyle wholeheartedly apologized to the Lord, to the churches in Hawaii and the Philippines, and to his physical family. He wept as he expressed how disappointed the Lord was in him and how his falling away had a devastating impact on so many peoples' faith.

217

Our dear brother Kyle Bartholomew
was tearfully restored!

Interestingly, after singing to Kyle, *We Love You With The Love Of The Lord,* and taking a fellowship break to welcome him back to the family, Kyle's father Jay – who is member of the Hilo Church – came up to Kip asking if he could address the church for five to ten minutes. After a quick "Nehemiah prayer," Kip said, "Sure!" So, after a song to gather everybody back, Kip introduced Jay to the church. Kip recorded Jay's poignant sharing in the *May 5, 2018 Good New Email:*

> *I want to share with you a true story, something that I witnessed about a month ago, but in fact, it is a parable. As I was walking, I heard the squawking of a large flock of mynah birds in a tree. All of a sudden, one of them flew off alone and immediately a huge hawk pounced on him, grabbing the mynah bird with his sharp talons! Then all*

*of the mynah birds in the tree squawked all the louder as they witnessed the hawk clutching one of their own! You may ask yourself why did the mynah bird fly off on its own? Well... Maybe it was arrogance? (Kyle shared during his restoration that the core sin that took him out was arrogance!) Maybe it was stupidity? Or maybe the mynah bird was just seeking a thrill?*

*Almost immediately after all the birds were screeching, four of the mynah birds came out of the tree and hit the hawk in rapid succession! Now you may be thinking, Why didn't more mynah birds come to the rescue? Well... Maybe they thought that the bird that flew out on its own was getting what he deserved? Or perhaps they did not help because they were just cowardly? Anyway, after the four birds hit the hawk, the hawk dropped the one mynah bird and that mynah bird flew quickly to safety back with the flock in the tree.*

*I believe the church is a family and for me, I can never give up on family. Let me just say, Kyle is not the only one who has struggled in this church and went away on his own. Don't look down on your brothers and sisters that stray like the one mynah bird, but with love and courage – no matter the price – go after them. Be true family! That's all I've got to say.*

Then Jay went back into the audience and sat down. The entire Hilo Church gave him a long-standing ovation!

Hawaiin Mynah Birds!

Another sign of the Year of Grace was on Sunday, September 23rd – the historic Signing Ceremony for the Memorandum of Understanding (MOU) of the "Chhem MERCY Orphanage" between the Cambodia Social Welfare Department and MERCY*worldwide!* Kip's first visit to Phnom Penh, Cambodia was in early 1997 to visit HOPE*worldwide's* new Sihanouk Hospital! At that time, Kip was deeply moved by the warmth and humility of the Cambodian people. In February 2001, he brought the ICOC World Sector Leaders to visit the HOPE Sihanouk Hospital and to preach at the then 300-member Phnom Penh ICOC. Now in 2018, Kip shared that "the city had changed so much – so modern, so much construction, and so little care for people."

Best of friends, Kip and Nick toured the
Sihanouk Hospital in September 2018!

The HOPE Sihanouk Hospital was famous in Cambodia.
Why so you may ask? In the late 70's, the Khmer Rouge –
under the cruel dictatorship of Pol Pot in a country of 11
million people – slaughtered two million innocents. For the
most part, this was a purposeful genocide of the intelligentsia
– doctors, politicians, educators, etc.

So, the HOPE Sihanouk Hospital set about to offer free
medical assistance, to give free medicines, and to train
doctors in a nation where they had been almost totally
eradicated. The Cambodian people were greatly moved by
HOPE's efforts, particularly the labors of our lead
Cambodian-disciple doctor – Dr. Tan Kim Meng! Sadly,
with the collapse of the ICOC and HOPE*worldwide* in the
2000's, when Kip visited the hospital on Saturday,
September 22nd, it was a barely functional hospital and in
great need of repair. Kip's heart ached as he witnessed a
decaying monument to a glorious but nearly forgotten past.
A few years earlier, Dr. Tan had been "unceremoniously
released from employment" at the hospital and set up a

private practice. Later Saturday, Kip visited Dr. Tan in his beautiful new clinic!

Kip and Nick visited Dr. Tan at his new clinic!

That Saturday afternoon, Kip accompanied by the Bordieris travelled to meet for the first time General Chhem – a one-star General in charge of Cambodia's Military Police, and the key overseer of what would be named the "Chhem MERCY Orphanage."

Sunday, the Phnom Penh Remnant Group had exactly 40 in attendance! Kip preached on The Dream, which was subtitled, What Can 12 Disciples Do, since the Phnom Penh Church now numbered 12 members! That lesson and the time that Kip spent with the remnant disciples so helped the Bordieris to solidify the sold-out foundation of the Phnom Penh Church.

That afternoon was the official MOU Signing Ceremony and Celebration Dinner! Humorously, Kip had thought that General Chhem had asked him on Saturday to do the prayer. However, at the Signing Ceremony, the General passed to Kip the "order of events." When Kip looked at the program, he was shocked to discover that he was scheduled to deliver the "Keynote Address!" Well, after a three-minute preparation, Kip spoke on dreaming, and Blady Perez did a terrific job translating him into Khmer!

Kip was "given the words to say" for the impromptu, but heart-moving Dedication Address!

Since, Kip was speaking to a predominantly Buddhist audience, he talked about how all that gathered that day were united in a common dream to change Phnom Penh, Cambodia, Southeast Asia and the world! He shared that "dreamers were people that did not see things as they are, but as they could be!" Then he illustrated this by sharing the moving account from the 1972 movie based on Cervante's *The Man Of La Mancha* about Eldonza the prostitute and Don Quixote, the old and crazy dreamer of a knight. When Don Quixote at their first meeting spoke to this woman of ill repute, he asked her name. She gruffly said Eldonza! Quixote pleasantly responded that her name was not (harsh-sounding) Eldonza, but (literally sweet) Dulcinea! By the end of the movie, she believed she was in fact "Dulcinea!"

Kip also held up General Chhem as an example of what an orphan can do if given love and opportunity, since he had been orphaned during the evil reign of the Khmer Rouge.

Kip closed with T. E. Lawrence's (Lawrence of Arabia) autobiographical quote, "All men dream but not equally. Those who dream by night. wake in the day to find that it was vanity; but the dreamers of the day are dangerous men [and women] for they may act on their dreams with open eyes to make it possible. This I did!" The General and the disciples expressed that it was one of the most moving speeches that they had ever heard!

The historic signing of the Memorandum
of Understanding by General
Chhem and Kip!

Following was the actual Signing of the Memorandum of Understanding! Ney Sakal (Board Member of the Cambodia Social Welfare Mission – CSWM – and Secretary of Finance of Cambodia) and Nick (President of MERCY*worldwide*) signed. Then a hush came over the crowd as General Chhem (Chairman of the Board of the CSWM) and Kip (Chairman of the Board of MERCY*worldwide*) signed!

MERCY's flagship project has become the Chhem
MERCY Orphanage!

After the signing pictures were taken, a fantastic Celebration
Dinner was served to all 58 orphans and to the 20 dignitaries!
Kip wrote in the *Good News Email* that the MOU Signing
was one of the highlights of his year! Pray for the orphanage
as this is MERCY's first Signature Project that MERCY is
supporting at $8,000 per month! Pray for the valiant
Bordieris who are "going third world" in their 50's! Pray for
the 58 orphans to become disciples! Pray for the Bordieris to
prioritize and raise the money for the many needed repairs
for the orphanage: bathrooms, kitchens, offices, air-
conditioning, etc. Pray for Blady & Cielo Perez who are
fluent in Khmer and are training in Manila to lead the Phnom
Penh Mission Team in June 2019!

General Chhemm and Kip were inspired by the
"Coca Cola Toast" given by the orphans
at the Celebration Dinner!

As I type these words, it is now mid-December 2018. Though the miraculous events of God's New Movement will continue into 2019 – The Year of Boldness, they will surely be recorded through many, many vehicles: Kip's exciting *Good News Emails*, ICC Hot News, the SoldOut Press International books, and the ever-increasing number of church bulletins, church websites and social media platforms. Therefore, this seemed a fitting time for me to conclude my account.

Kip & Elena will be busy planning and preaching at the now 10 Geographic Missions Conferences outside the United States as there will not be another GLC until August 2020. The 2019 Geographic Missions Conferences include:

1. **The South American Missions Conference**
   Santiago, Chile – February 1-3, 2019
2. **The Eurasian Missions Conference**
   Moscow, Russia – May 3-5, 2019

3. **The Pacific Rim Missions Conference**
   Manila, Philippines – June 13-16, 2019
4. **The African Missions Conference**
   Lagos, Nigeria – June 28-30, 2019
5. **The Latin American Missions Conference**
   Mexico City, Mexico – July 18-21, 2019
6. **The new Caribbean Missions Conference**
   Port-au-Prince, Haiti – October 4-6, 2019
7. **The European Missions Conference**
   London, England – October 24-27, 2019
8. **The Austral-China Missions Conference**
   Sydney, Australia – November 1-3, 2019
9. **The South Asia Missions Conference**
   New Delhi, India – November 14-17, 2019
10. **The new Middle East Missions Conference**
    Dubai, UAE – December 6-8, 2019

Today on December 16, 2018, my awesome wife Tracy and I were sent out by the Spirit to lead the planting of the 20th OPERATION Eagle Planting – Atlanta, Georgia! Please pray for us, the 20 courageous disciples that God gathered from every corner of the United States and the thirsty remnant waiting in Atlanta for revival! Indeed, it has been the honor of my life to live in the midst of these times and to be able to record these historic events!

And to God be all the glory!

The motto of the zealous Atlanta Mission Team is PEACH:
Powerfully Evangelizing All Creatures under Heaven!

The McKeans and the Hardings have pledged to each
other, "We are family… to the end!"

# EPILOGUE

In May 2007, Kip and Elena McKean – alongside 40 other disciples from Portland – planted the City of Angels International Christian Church, which now has 1,300 at their Sunday Services! However, the true impact of Kip's leadership must be measured not only in the multiplying of disciples in Los Angeles, but in the multiplying of churches planted from LA and the ensuring generations of church plantings. When one counts all of these churches, in just 11 years' time, the Lord used the original 42 members of the City of Angels Mission Team to multiply into over 7,000 disciples!

During the 10th Anniversary Celebration Weekend of the City of Angels Church, 175 key leaders from around the world gathered for an evening cruise to honor the "42" who planted the City of Angels Church!

Overall, the SoldOut Movement is now present on all six populated countries of the world! Counting both "church plantings" and "remnant groups," God's New Movement collectively numbers almost 100 congregations in 38 countries: Australia, Bolivia, Brazil, Burkina Faso, Cambodia, Cameroon, Canada, Chile, China, Colombia, Curacao, Democratic Republic of Congo, Dominican Republic, Ecuador, England, Ethiopia, France, Haiti, India, Ivory Coast, Kenya, Malawi, Mexico, Mozambique, New

Zealand, Nigeria, Peru, Philippines, Qatar, Russia, Saudi Arabia, Sierra Leone, South Africa, Sweden, Uganda, Ukraine, United Arab Emirates, and the United States of America... and counting!

Kip's uncompromising call from the Scriptures to all who would follow Jesus has remained the same for his 43 years in the ministry: "Go anywhere, do anything, give up everything." For he deeply believes that Jesus' dream for "the evangelization of the nations in this generation" can and only will be accomplished through a movement composed only of sold-out disciples! Most mornings *while it is still dark,* Kip prays that before he dies that the Lord will allow him to write as Paul did, *"All over the world this Gospel is bearing fruit and... has been proclaimed to every creature under Heaven."* And to God be all the glory!

Kip and Elena climbed Diamond Head Mountain in Hawaii
and prayed for the the evangelization of the nations
in this generation!

The most detailed accounting of the continuing legacy of *The Chronicles of Modern Day Christianity* can be found in the SoldOut Movement's Good News Emails at:

http://www.caicc.net/category/articles/good-news-email/

Ronald C. Harding, Jr

December 16, 2018

# APPENDIX: FIRST PRINCIPLES
### by Dr. Kip McKean

*"For when by reason of the time you ought to be teachers, you... need to have someone teach you the rudiments of the first principles of the oracles of God... Therefore leaving the doctrine of the first principles of Christ, let us press on to perfection – not laying again a foundation... of faith toward God, of the teaching of baptisms, of laying on of hands, of resurrection of the dead and of eternal judgment. This will we do!"* **Hebrews 5:12; 6:1-3 (WEV)**

Originally, the First Principle Studies were written in 1980, while I served the Lord during the formative early days of the Boston Church of Christ. They were revised in 2003 and 2006 to meet the needs and to confront the challenges of the Portland International Church of Christ. In Los Angeles in 2009, 2012 and 2018, I made a few more modifications. As of today, these same First Principles Studies are being taught to all the new disciples of the City of Angels International Christian Church. God has greatly blessed these lessons as they have been translated into over 20 languages around the world. May the Lord continue to "solidify, unify and multiply" SoldOut disciples everywhere for the evangelization of all the nations in this generation! And to God be the glory!

Dr. Kip McKean

August 8, 2018

# COURSE INFORMATION

1.  This course should take a high priority in your day as it is geared to help you grasp a firmer hold on God's Word and to deepen your understanding of His will for your life.

2.  Each session two new Scriptures should be memorized for a written or verbal quiz at the beginning of each class.

3.  Each study's content and order of Scriptures should also be memorized for the quiz.

4.  Each student is required to memorize the names of all the books of the Bible.

5.  Sign up for the Good News Emails at CAICC.net by Session 2.

6.  Read Ron Harding's *The Chronicles of Modern-Day Christianity* by Session 8.

7.  An outline of the book of Acts will be turned in by session 11. Each student is required to memorize two points from each chapter in the book of Acts.

# OUTLINE OF CLASSES

| | |
|---|---|
| Session 1 | Introduction and Seeking God |
| Session 2 | The Word of God |
| Session 3 | Discipleship |
| Session 4 | The Coming of the Kingdom |
| Session 5 | Light and Darkness |
| Session 6 | New Testament Conversion |
| Session 7 | The Cross |
| Session 8 | The Baptism with the Holy Spirit |
| Session 9 | The Miraculous Gifts of the Holy Spirit |
| Session 10 | The Church |

# SUGGESTED READING LIST

These books are recommended as thought-provoking and informative tools to be used in gaining insights into God's Word. In no way are they suggested to be biblically correct on all doctrinal points.

| | |
|---|---|
| Chapman: | The Five Love Languages |
| Coleman: | The Master Plan of Evangelism |
| Edwards: | The Tale of Three Kings |
| Rivers: | Voice in the Wind |
| Taylor: | The Disciplined Life |

# SCRIPTURE MEMORY

"But in your hearts set apart Christ as Lord. Always be prepared to give an answer to everyone who asks you to give the reason for the hope that you have. But do this with gentleness and respect." 1 Peter 3:15

**Session 1**
Jeremiah 29:11
Matthew 6:33

**Session 2**
John 8:31-32
Philippians 4:13

**Session 3**
Mark 1:17
John 13:34-35

**Session 4**
Acts 2:38
Philippians 4:4

**Session 5**
Ezekiel 18:20
Galatians 1:8

**Session 6**
Matthew 22:37-39
John 15:8

**Session 7**
Matthew 28:18-20
Luke 19:10

**Session 8**
Hebrews 10:24-25
1 John 1:9

**Session 9**
Hebrews 12:15
Hebrews 13:17

234

# INTRODUCTION TO THE COURSE

1. **Course Requirements**

2. **Purpose of First Principles Class**
   **A. Solidify** – Hebrews 6:1-3
   **B. Unify** – John 13:34-35
   **Multiply** – Matthew 28:18-20

   **How to win people to Christ**

   **A.** Build a good friendship
      i. Spend time
   Have discussions

   **B.** Find out their background
      i. Life story (also share yours)
   Present beliefs about God, Christ and the Bible

   **C.** Ask your friend to study the Bible with you.

   **D.** Buy a Bible as a gift
      i. A readable version
   Inscribe a meaningful thought

   **E.** If they are an unbeliever about Jesus or if they
      are unclear about Him then…
      i. Study the book of John
   Purpose (**John 20:30-31**)

   If they believe in Jesus start with the Seeking God
   Study

3. Have a Christian friend you are discipling in on the
   study as well. Take concise notes for your non-
   Christian friend, so they can go back and review
   what has been studied.

# SEEKING GOD

1. **Psalm 119:1-2**
   A. Blessed means happy (superlatively happy)
   B. Happiness is not the goal of one who seeks God but the "by-product"
   C. To seek God you must do it with all your heart
   D. Seeking God means to "keep His statutes"

2. **Matthew 6:25-34**
   A. Do not worry – ironic – can not add a single hour to your life
   B. God knows your needs
   C. Seek first His kingdom and righteousness
   D. Then God will give you everything you need

3. **Acts 17:26-28**
   A. God determines the times and places each person lives
   B. He does this so men will seek Him, reach out for Him and find Him
   C. He is not far from anyone
   D. A Christian meeting you is not by chance – but of God

4. **John 4:23-24**
   A. God seeks men (Acts 17 taught men must seek God)
   B. Men who want to worship Him in spirit and in truth

5. **Acts 17:10-12**
   A. Read and study the Bible for your own convictions
   B. Study daily

6. **Jeremiah 29:11-14**
   A. God has an individual plan for your life
   B. A plan to prosper you – with hope and a future
   C. You will find God when you seek Him with all your heart

7. **Acts 8:26-39**
   A. The angels and the Holy Spirit are helping to get you to God
   B. Do not be afraid to ask questions about life or the Bible – be humble
   C. You need someone to explain the Bible to you
   D. You will be "rejoicing" when you find God

8. **Matthew 7:7-8**
   A. Seek and God guarantees you will find Him
   B. Ask God for help

# THE WORD OF GOD

1. **2 Timothy 3:16-17**
   A. All Scripture is inspired by God
   B. It is to be applied to our lives

2. **Hebrews 4:12-13**
   A. The Word is relevant
   B. The Word cuts (hurts)-compare it to a scalpel
   C. It is good to be cut because it cuts the "cancer" (sin) out

3. **2 Peter 1: 20-21**
   A. There is no private interpretation of the Bible
   B. The Holy Spirit inspired the men who wrote the books of the Bible

4. **John 8:31-32**
   A. Intellectual belief is not enough-nor can we go by our feelings
   B. Everyone must hold on to and follow the teachings of Jesus to be a true disciple
   C. Sincerity does not equal truth
   D. Religious people can be wrong

5. **Matthew 15:1-9**
   A. Do not go by traditions or creeds
   B. Worship by traditions (which supercede the Word of God) is worship in vain

6. **1 Timothy 4:16**
   A. Watch your life and doctrine closely-they are inseparable
   B. Which is more important, life or doctrine? Neither-an airplane with only one wing cannot fly

238

C. Why is it so important to learn and to teach and to live the right doctrine? To save yourself and those who hear you

7. **Acts 17:10-12**
   A. Must check what religious leaders say
   B. Your challenge: Read and study the Bible every day!

8. **James 1:22-25**
   A. The Word of God is a mirror
   B. Do not forget what you see – "do what it says"

9. **John 12:48**
   A. Why study the Bible? The Word will judge us
   B. Decision: Will I live by the Bible or my feelings, traditions, needs, etc.?

# DISCIPLESHIP

**Introduction: Matthew 28:18-20**

  **A.** What does Jesus want everybody to become?

  **B.** Which is the more popular term -"Disciple" or
"Christian?" The word "Christian" only appears
three times in the New Testament. It is the name
those in the world gave the disciples, seven years
after the church began. (**Acts 11:19-26**) The word
"Disciple" occurs over 270 times in the New
Testament.

  **C.** SAVED=CHRISTIAN=DISCIPLE

  **D.** Jesus came to make disciples. Only baptized
disciples will be saved.

LET'S HAVE JESUS DEFINE DISCIPLE, THUS DEFINING WHO
IS A TRUE CHRISTIAN

**1. Mark 1:14-18**

  **A.** Calling of the first disciples

  **B.** Come follow me (Christ)

  **C.** Fishers of men -Jesus gave these first disciples the
real purpose for living

  **D.** Immediately

**2. Luke 9:23-26**

  **A.** If any man...

  **B.** Deny self. Notice Christ in the garden (**Matthew
26:36-39**, "Not my will, but your will.") Do not
give in to moods

  **C.** Carry the cross - daily

  **D.** Gain world ... forfeit soul. Lose your life for Jesus
... save it

**3. Luke 14:25-33**

A. If any man...
B. Count the cost (v. 28-30)
C. Consider the alternatives (v. 31-32)
D. Love Christ more than any person (v. 26)
E. Persecutions (v. 27)
F. Everything, not just anything (v. 33)

## 4. Luke 11:1-4
A. Must learn to pray - disciples saw the strength Jesus received from the Father
B. Daily personal relationship with God (v. 3); daily prayer

## 5. John 13:34-35
A. Love one another
B. Be an active part of the fellowship

## 6. Matthew 28:18-20
A. Command - make disciples (given to all)
B. Who is a candidate for baptism? People who make the decision to be a disciple
C. You need someone to disciple you to maturity in Christ
D. This is the only way to save the world!

| Year | Preacher | Disciple |
|------|----------|----------|
| 1 | 365 | 2 |
| 2 | 730 | 4 |
| 3 | 1095 | 8 |
| 13 | 4745 | 8192 |
| 32 | 11,680 | the world, 10 billion plus |

**Conclusion Questions:** Am I a disciple? Am I a Christian? Am I saved? What do I need to do to become a disciple?

# THE COMING OF THE KINGDOM

In this study you will see the continuity of the Old and New Testaments.

Questions:     What is the Kingdom of God?  When did it come?

1.  Old Testament Predictions of the Kingdom (The height of Israel's glory was under the kingship of David approximately 1000 B.C.)
    A. **Isaiah 2:1-4 (750 B.C.)**
       1. Last days
       2. All nations
       3. Jerusalem
    B. **Daniel 2:31-45 (550 B.C.)**
       1. Daniel interprets King Nebuchadnezzar's dream
       2. Empires
       3. Babylonian: gold
       4. Medo-Persian: silver
       5. Alexander the Great: bronze
       6. Roman: iron (iron and clay)
    C. Rock – cut out not by human hands (therefore God)
    D. Rock becomes huge mountain – filled the whole earth
       1. Kingdom that will never be destroyed (v. 44)

2.  New Testament Predictions of the Kingdom
    A. John the Baptist (**25 A.D.**)
       1. Kingdom is near (**Matthew 3:1-6**)
    B. Jesus (**30 A.D.**)
       1. Kingdom is near (**Matthew 4:17**)
       2. Kingdom will come in the lifetime of some of the disciples (**Mark 9:1**)
       3. Kingdom will come with power (**Mark 9:1**)

242

     4.  Kingdom entered by new birth (**John 3:1-7**)
     5.  Kingdom is within you (**Luke 17:20-21**)
     6.  Peter has the keys (**Matthew 16:13-19**). Church and the Kingdom are the same and will be built on the truth that Jesus is the Christ (**1 Corinthians 3:11**).
     7.  Joseph of Arimathea was still waiting for the Kingdom when Jesus died (**Luke 23:50-51**).
     8.  Repentance and forgiveness of sins will be preached first in Jerusalem to all nations (**Luke 24:44-49**).

3.  Fulfillment of the Old and New Testament Predictions **Acts 1-2 (33 A.D.)**
    **A.**  Last days (**Acts 2:17**)
      1.  **Isaiah 2:2**
    **B.**  All nations (**Acts 2:5**)
      1.  **Isaiah 2:2**
      2.  **Luke 24:47**
    **C.**  Jerusalem (**Acts 2:5**)
      1.  **Isaiah 2:3**
      2.  **Luke 24:44-49**
    **D.**  Eternal kingdom (**Acts 2:37-42**)
      1.  **Daniel 2:31-45**
    **E.**  Date of coming approximately **33 A.D.** (**Acts 1-2**)
      1.  Old testament prophecy
      2.  John the Baptist "is near" (**Matthew 3:1-2**)
      3.  Jesus-"is near" (**Matthew 4:17**)
    **F.**  Lifetime (**Acts 2:14**)
      1.  **Mark 9:1**
      2.  "Some"-Judas died (**Acts 1:18-19**)
    **G.**  Power (**Acts 1:8, Acts 2:1-4**)
      1.  **Mark 9:1**http://bible.gospelcom.net/bible?Mark+9:1
    **H.**  New birth (**Acts 2:38**)
      1.  Water and Spirit (**John 3:1-7**)
    **I.**  Kingdom within (**Acts 2:37**)

        **1. Luke 17:20 - 21**
    **J.** Peter with the keys (**Acts 2:14, 38**)
        **1. Matthew 16:19**
    **K.** Repentance and forgiveness of sin (**Acts 2:38**)
        **1. Luke 24:44-49**

**4. Conclusion**
    **A.** The church is the kingdom of God on earth established in approximately **33 A.D.**
    **B. Acts 2:42** As citizens of the kingdom and members of the body (the church), we must be devoted to:
        **1.** Doctrine
        **2.** Fellowship
        **3.** Breaking Bread
        **4.** Prayer
    **C. Matthew 6:33** We must seek his kingdom first. Ask them to commit themselves to at least Sunday services and Midweek services.

# LIGHT AND DARKNESS

**Introduction: 1 Peter 2:9-10**

| Darkness | Light |
|---|---|
| Not a people of God | People of God |
| No Mercy | Mercy |
| | |
| Lost | Saved |
| Not a Christian | Christian |
| Not a Disciple | Disciple |

**A.** Every person is either in the darkness or the light. There is no twilight zone.

**B.** Where are you?

**1. Darkness**

**A. Isaiah 59:1-2**

    **1.** Sin separates us from God.

**WALL**

| DARKNESS MAN | | LIGHT GOD |
|---|---|---|

**SIN**

    **2.** In order for a man to have a relationship with God the wall must be broken down-sin must be forgiven.

    **3.** The point in time sin is forgiven is the point in time a person is saved.

**B. Romans 3:23-25**

    **1.** Who has sinned? Everyone!

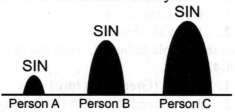

SIN    SIN    SIN

Person A    Person B    Person C

2. Who is further away from God, a person
who sins a little or a person who sins a lot?
All are equal, all lost. Therefore, a good
moral life does not save you. You cannot
earn your salvation by your good deeds.
3. Faith in the blood of Jesus saves you (v. 25).
C. What is Sin?
   1. **Galatians 5:19-21** (sins of commission)
   2. **2 Timothy 3:1-5** (sins of commission)
   3. **James 4:17** (sins of omission)
D. What is the eternal consequence of sin? **Romans
   6:23**

| WAGES OF SIN | GIFT OF GOD |
|---|---|
| Death | Eternal Life |
| Hell | Heaven |
| Darkness | Light |

2. **Light**
   A. **John 3:1-7** - Born again (v. 3), born of water and
      spirit (v. 5), born again (v. 7).
   B. Personal decision as an adult
   C. What message must one believe to be in the light (to
      be saved?) **Acts 2:22-24.**
      1. Jesus is from God (v. 22).
      2. Jesus raised physically from the dead (v.
         24).
      3. Everyone is responsible for the crucifixion
         of Christ (v. 23). All have sinned (**Romans
         3:23**).
   D. Response of people **Acts 2:37**
      1. Cut to the heart
      2. What shall we do?
   E. Once the people believed, what did they do? **Acts
      2:38-42**
      1. Repent (Greek = to turn)
      2. Be baptized (Greek = to be immersed).

246

      **a.** Sin forgiven. Therefore, this is the point in time a person is saved.

      **b.** Holy Spirit given to each who responded-power to live as God commands.

**F.** Baptism **Romans 6:1-4**

Baptism is the sharing (a participation) in the death, burial and resurrection of Christ. (More than just a symbol.)

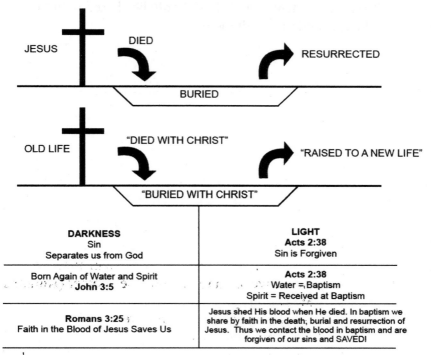

| | |
|---|---|
| **DARKNESS**<br>Sin<br>Separates us from God | **LIGHT**<br>**Acts 2:38**<br>Sin is Forgiven |
| Born Again of Water and Spirit<br>**John 3:5** | **Acts 2:38**<br>Water = Baptism<br>Spirit = Received at Baptism |
| **Romans 3:25**<br>Faith in the Blood of Jesus Saves Us | Jesus shed His blood when He died. In baptism we share by faith in the death, burial and resurrection of Jesus. Thus we contact the blood in baptism and are forgiven of our sins and SAVED! |

### 3. Traditions/False Doctrines-Matthew 15:6-9

   **A.** Infant Baptism

      **1.** Personal faith is needed (**Colossians 2:12**).

      **2.** Began approximately third century A.D.

      **3.** Original sin

         a. **Ezekiel 18:20**

         b. Became "church doctrine" in 549 A.D.

247

**B.** Praying Jesus into your heart

    **1.** **Revelation 3:20** - taken out of context. This verse is addressed to Christians.

    **2.** Began in the early 1800s in America.

## 4. Sinful nature

Suggest to the individual with whom you are studying that he or she write out and be specific about various sins they have committed during their life. This is so that they might see the gravity and magnitude of their sin. This is confidential and should only be shared with those who are studying with the person.

# NEW TESTAMENT CONVERSION

1. **THE MAJOR CONVERSIONS IN ACTS**
   **A. Conversions**
      1. **Acts 2:36-47** First Christian in Jerusalem
      2. **Acts 8:26-39** Ethiopian Eunuch
      3. **Acts 16:22-34** Philippian jailer and his family
      4. **Acts 9:1-22** Paul
         **Acts 22:3-16** Paul
      5. **Acts 18:24-26** Apollos
      6. **Acts 19:1-5** Ephesians
   **B. Questions concerning Conversions**
      1. What was preached?
      2. What was the person's (people's) response to the message?
      3. How long did the person (people) take to make the decision?
      4. What was their response after baptism?

2. **REFUTING FALSE DOCTRINES**
   **A.** "Pray Jesus into your heart": This phrase is never mentioned in the Bible. People may use **Revelation 3:20** about Jesus knocking at the door, however, you must examine the Scripture in context. This scripture does not teach how to become a Christian and be saved, but how to come back to God after becoming lukewarm. It is addressed to disciples who already responded to Christ in faith, repentance, confession and baptism. "Accept Jesus into your heart": (same teaching as praying Jesus into your heart-just different terminology.) Based on **Romans 10:9**. You must look at scripture in context. Paul is addressing the problem of the Israelites: unbelief that Jesus was the Christ, the Son of God. Read further on to **Romans 10:13**. When do you call on the name of the Lord? At baptism (**Acts 22:16**).

**B.** Infant baptism: A baby cannot have faith, and since we are baptized through faith in the power of God (**Colossians 2:12**), babies cannot be baptized. Original sin: **Ezekiel 18:20** teaches there is no original sin; each person is responsible for his own actions and will be judged accordingly. Therefore babies are born sinless and will be saved if they die.

**C.** "Baptism does not save you": **1 Peter 3:21** says that baptism does save you through the resurrection of Jesus Christ. **Acts 2:38** teaches that sin is forgiven at baptism-one is saved at the point sin is forgiven.

**D.** "Baptism is a work-yet we are saved by faith" (**Ephesians 2:8**): **Colossians 2:12** teaches we are saved by faith-in the working of God at baptism.

**E.** "Baptism is an outward sign of an inward grace": **Romans 6:2-4** states that baptism is an actual participation in the death, burial and resurrection of Christ. It is not merely a sign, seal or symbol.

**F.** "Baptism isn't important, after all, look at what Paul said about it in **1 Corinthians 1:17**": Paul does not diminish the importance of baptism here. (Paul himself was baptized to have his sins forgiven in **Acts 22:16**.) In context (read **1 Corinthians 1:10-17**), he makes the point that he does not want people following men (denominationalism). He mentions baptism several times in the passage.

**G.** "The thief on the cross was not baptized and Jesus told him that they would see each other in paradise": Jesus had not even died yet, and baptism is participating in his death (**Romans 6:2-4**); also on earth, he had the power to forgive sins (**Matthew 9:2-6**).

**H.** "Believers baptism": This is baptism as an adult, but is not done in conjunction with the understanding that one is being saved at this point in time (**John 3:5, Acts 2:38**). "Retroactive understanding" is not sufficient for salvation.

# THE CROSS

1. **Passion Account**
   Read **Matthew 26:31 - 28:10**.
   Suggested Reading Intervals:
   **26:31-35 27:27-31**
   **26:36-46 27:32-44**
   **26:47-56 27:45-56**
   **26:57-68 27:57-61**
   **26:69-75 27:62-66**
   **27:1-10 28:1-10**
   **27:11-26**

2. **Physical Death**
   Read the medical account of Jesus' physical death.

3. **Personal Responsibility**
   A. Remember there were many others who died by crucifixion in the first century. It was not that Jesus was painfully crucified that makes him unique-it was that he was crucified for you, in your place. He died on the cross for you.
   B. **Romans 3:23**
   C. **Isaiah 59:1-2**
   D. **Matthew 27:46**
   E. Share the sins that you committed before being baptized and your feelings of being forgiven at baptism. Ask the person with whom you are studying to share and confess their sins.
   F. **Isaiah 53:4-6** (substitute your name).

# THE MEDICAL ACCOUNT OF THE CRUCIFIXION OF CHRIST

**Dr. C. Truman Davis**
A Physician Analyzes the Crucifixion
by Dr. C. Truman Davis

About a decade ago, reading Jim Bishop's The Day Christ Died, I realized that I had for years taken the Crucifixion more or less for granted -- that I had grown callous to its horror by a too easy familiarity with the grim details and a too distant friendship with our Lord. It finally occurred to me that, though a physician, I didn't even know the actual immediate cause of death. The Gospel writers don't help us much on this point, because crucifixion and scourging were so common during their lifetime that they apparently considered a detailed description unnecessary. So we have only the concise words of the Evangelists: "Pilate, having scourged Jesus, delivered Him to them to be crucified -- and they crucified Him."

I have no competence to discuss the infinite psychic and spiritual suffering of the Incarnate God atoning for the sins of fallen man. But it seemed to me that as a physician I might pursue the physiological and anatomical aspects of our Lord's passion at some detail. What did the body of Jesus of Nazareth actually endure during those hours of torture?

This led me first to a study of the practice of crucifixion itself; that is, torture and execution by fixation to a cross.

Apparently, the first known practice of crucifixion was by the Persians. Alexander and his generals brought it back to the Mediterranean world -- to Egypt and to Carthage. The Romans apparently learned the practice from the Carthaginians and (as with almost everything the Romans did) rapidly developed a very high degree of efficiency and skill at it. A number of Roman authors (Livy, Cicero, Tacitus) comment on crucifixion, and several innovations, modifications, and variations are described in the ancient literature.

For instance, the upright portion of the cross (or stipes) could have the cross-arm (or patibulum) attached two or three feet below its top in what we commonly think of as the Latin cross. The most common form used in our Lord's day, however, was the Tau cross, shaped like our T. In this cross the patibulum was placed in a notch at the top of the stipes. There is archeological evidence that it was on this type of cross that Jesus was crucified.

Without any historical or biblical proof, Medieval and Renaissance painters have given us our picture of Christ carrying the entire cross. But the upright post, or stipes, was generally fixed permanently in the ground at the site of execution and the condemned man was forced to carry the patibulum, weighing about 110 pounds, from the prison to the place of execution.

Many of the painters and most of the sculptors of crucifixion, also show the nails through the palms. Historical Roman accounts and experimental work have established that the nails were driven between the small bones of the wrists (radial and ulna) and not through the palms. Nails driven through the palms will strip out between the fingers when made to support the weight of the human body. The misconception may have come about through a misunderstanding of Jesus' words to Thomas, "Observe my hands." Anatomists, both modern and ancient, have always considered the wrist as part of the hand.

A titulus, or small sign, stating the victim's crime was usually placed on a staff, carried at the front of the procession from the prison, and later nailed to the cross so that it extended above the head. This sign with its staff nailed to the top of the cross would have given it somewhat the characteristic form of the Latin cross.

But, of course, the physical passion of the Christ began in Gethsemane. Of the many aspects of this initial suffering, the one of greatest physiological interest is the bloody sweat. It is interesting that St. Luke, the physician, is the only one to mention this. He says, "And being in Agony, He prayed the longer. And His sweat became as drops of blood, trickling down upon the ground."

Every ruse (trick) imaginable has been used by modern scholars to explain away this description, apparently under the mistaken impression that this just doesn't happen. A great deal of effort could have been saved had the doubters consulted the medical literature. Though very rare, the phenomenon of Hematidrosis, or bloody sweat, is well documented. Under great emotional stress of the kind our Lord suffered, tiny capillaries in the sweat glands can break, thus mixing blood with sweat. This process might well have produced marked weakness and possible shock.

After the arrest in the middle of the night, Jesus was next brought before the Sanhedrin and Caiphus, the High Priest; it is here that the first physical trauma was inflicted. A soldier struck Jesus across the face for remaining silent when questioned by Caiphus. The palace guards then blind-folded Him and mockingly taunted Him to identify them as they each passed by, spat upon Him, and struck Him in the face.

In the early morning, battered and bruised, dehydrated, and exhausted from a sleepless night, Jesus is taken across the Praetorium of the Fortress Antonia, the seat of government of the Procurator of Judea, Pontius Pilate. You are, of course, familiar with Pilate's action in attempting to pass responsibility to Herod Antipas, the Tetrarch of Judea. Jesus apparently suffered no physical mistreatment at the hands of Herod and was returned to Pilate. It was the, in response to the cries of the mob, that Pilate ordered Bar-Abbas released and condemned Jesus to scourging and crucifixion.

There is much disagreement among authorities about the unusual scourging as a prelude to crucifixion. Most Roman writers from this period do not associate the two. Many scholars believe that Pilate originally ordered Jesus scourged as his full punishment and that the death sentence by crucifixion came only in response to the taunt by the mob that the Procurator was not properly defending Caesar against this pretender who allegedly claimed to be the King of the Jews.

Preparations for the scourging were carried out when the Prisoner was stripped of His clothing and His hands tied to a post above His head. It is doubtful the Romans would have made any attempt to follow the Jewish law in this matter, but the Jews had an ancient law prohibiting more than forty lashes.

The Roman legionnaire steps forward with the flagrum (or flagellum) in his hand. This is a short whip consisting of several heavy, leather thongs with two small balls of lead attached near the ends of each. The heavy whip is brought down with full force again and again across Jesus' shoulders, back, and legs. At first the thongs cut through the skin only. Then, as the blows continue, they cut deeper into the subcutaneous tissues, producing first an oozing of blood from the capillaries and veins of the skin, and finally spurting arterial bleeding from vessels in the underlying muscles.

The small balls of lead first produce large, deep bruises which are broken open by subsequent blows. Finally the skin of the back is hanging in long ribbons and the entire area is an unrecognizable mass of torn, bleeding tissue. When it is determined by the centurion in charge that the prisoner is near death, the beating is finally stopped.

The half-fainting Jesus is then untied and allowed to slump to the stone pavement, wet with His own blood. The Roman soldiers see a great joke in this provincial Jew claiming to be king. They throw a robe across His shoulders and place a stick in His hand for a scepter. They still need a crown to make their travesty complete. Flexible branches covered with long thorns (commonly used in bundles for firewood) are plaited into the shape of a crown and this is pressed into His scalp. Again there is copious bleeding, the scalp being one of the most vascular areas of the body.

After mocking Him and striking Him across the face, the soldiers take the stick from His hand and strike Him across the head, driving the thorns deeper into His scalp. Finally, they tire of their sadistic sport and the robe is torn from His back. Already having adhered to the clots of blood and serum in the wounds, its removal causes excruciating pain just as in the careless removal of a surgical bandage, and almost as though He were again being whipped the wounds once more begin to bleed.

In deference to Jewish custom, the Romans return His garments. The heavy patibulum of the cross is tied across His shoulders, and the procession of the condemned Christ, two thieves, and the execution detail of Roman soldiers headed by a centurion begins its slow journey along the Via Dolorosa. In spite of His efforts to walk erect, the weight of the heavy wooden beam, together with the shock produced by copious blood loss, is too much. He stumbles and falls. The rough wood of the beam gouges into the lacerated skin and muscles of the shoulders. He tries to rise, but human muscles have been pushed beyond their endurance.

The centurion, anxious to get on with the crucifixion, selects a stalwart North African onlooker, Simon of Cyrene, to carry the cross. Jesus follows, still bleeding and sweating the cold, clammy sweat of shock, until the 650 yard journey from the fortress Antonia to Golgotha is finally completed.

Jesus is offered wine mixed with myrrh, a mild analgesic mixture. He refuses to drink. Simon is ordered to place the patibulum on the ground and Jesus quickly thrown backward with His shoulders against the wood. The legionnaire feels for the depression at the front of the wrist. He drives a heavy, square, wrought-iron nail through the wrist and deep into the wood. Quickly, he moves to the other side and repeats the action being careful not to pull the arms to tightly, but to allow some flexion and movement. The patibulum is then lifted in place at the top of the stipes and the titulus reading "Jesus of Nazareth, King of the Jews" is nailed in place.

The left foot is now pressed backward against the right foot, and with both feet extended, toes down, a nail is driven through the arch of each, leaving the knees moderately flexed. The Victim is now crucified. As He slowly sags down with more weight on the nails in the wrists excruciating pain shoots along the fingers and up the arms to explode in the brain -- the nails in the writs are putting pressure on the median nerves. As He pushes Himself upward to avoid this stretching torment, He places His full weight on the nail through His feet. Again there is the searing agony of the nail tearing through the nerves between the metatarsal bones of the feet.

At this point, as the arms fatigue, great waves of cramps sweep over the muscles, knotting them in deep, relentless, throbbing pain. With these cramps comes the inability to push Himself upward. Hanging by his arms, the pectoral muscles are paralyzed and the intercostal muscles are unable to act. Air can be drawn into the lungs, but cannot be exhaled. Jesus fights to raise Himself in order to get even one short breath. Finally, carbon dioxide builds up in the lungs and in the blood stream and the cramps partially subside. Spasmodically, he is able to push Himself upward to exhale and bring in the life-giving oxygen. It was undoubtedly during these periods that He uttered the seven short sentences recorded:

The first, looking down at the Roman soldiers throwing dice for His seamless garment, "Father, forgive them for they know not what they do."

The second, to the penitent thief, "Today thou shalt be with me in Paradise."

The third, looking down at the terrified, grief-stricken adolescent John -- the beloved Apostle -- he said, "Behold thy mother." Then, looking to His mother Mary, "Woman behold thy son."

The fourth cry is from the beginning of the 22nd Psalm, "My God, my God, why has thou forsaken me?"

Hours of limitless pain, cycles of twisting, joint-rending cramps, intermittent partial asphyxiation, searing pain where tissue is torn from His lacerated back as He moves up and down against the rough timber. Then another agony begins...A terrible crushing pain deep in the chest as the pericardium slowly fills with serum and begins to compress the heart.

One remembers again the 22nd Psalm, the 14th verse: "I am poured out like water, and all my bones are out of joint; my heart is like wax; it is melted in the midst of my bowels."

It is now almost over. The loss of tissue fluids has reached a critical level; the compressed heart is struggling to pump heavy, thick, sluggish blood into the tissue; the tortured lungs are making a frantic effort to gasp in small gulps of air. The markedly dehydrated tissues send their flood of stimuli to the brain.

Jesus gasps His fifth cry, "I thirst."

One remembers another verse from the prophetic 22nd Psalm: "My strength is dried up like a potsherd; and my tongue cleaveth to my jaws; and thou has brought me into the dust of death."

A sponge soaked in posca, the cheap, sour wine which is the staple drink of the Roman legionaries, is lifted to His lips. He apparently doesn't take any of the liquid. The body of Jesus is now in extremes, and He can feel the chill of death creeping through His tissues. This realization brings out His sixth words, possibly little more than a tortured whisper, "It is finished." His mission of atonement has completed. Finally He can allow his body to die.

With one last surge of strength, he once again presses His torn feet against the nail, straightens His legs, takes a deeper breath, and utters His seventh and last cry, "Father! Into thy hands I commit my spirit."

The rest you know. In order that the Sabbath not be profaned, the Jews asked that the condemned men be dispatched and removed from the crosses. The common method of ending a crucifixion was by crurifracture, the breaking of the bones of the legs. This prevented the victim from pushing himself upward; thus the tension could not be relieved from the muscles of the chest and rapid suffocation occurred. The legs of the two thieves were broken, but when the soldiers came to Jesus they saw that this was unnecessary.

Apparently to make doubly sure of death, the legionnaire drove his lance through the fifth interspace between the ribs, upward through the pericardium and into the heart. The 34th verse of the 19th chapter of the Gospel according to St. John reports: "And immediately there came out blood and water." That is, there was an escape of water fluid from the sac surrounding the heart, giving postmortem evidence that Our Lord died not the usual crucifixion death by suffocation, but of heart failure due to shock and constriction of the heart by fluid in the pericardium.

Thus we have had our glimpse -- including the medical evidence -- of that epitome of evil which man has exhibited toward Man and toward God. It has been a terrible sight, and more than enough to leave us despondent and depressed. How grateful we can be that we have the great sequel in the infinite mercy of God toward man -- at once the miracle of the atonement and the expectation of the triumphant Easter morning.

From New Wine Magazine, April 1982. Originally published in Arizona Medicine, March 1965, Arizona Medical Association.

# BAPTISM WITH THE HOLY SPIRIT

**Introduction:** Jesus was given the Spirit in full measure, no limit (**John 3:34**). There are three measures of the Holy Spirit:

## 1. The indwelling of the Holy Spirit

    **A.** Received at baptism (**Acts 2:38**)

## 2. The baptism with the Holy Spirit

    **A.** Characteristics in **Acts 2** and **Acts 10**

        1. Promise (not command), **Acts 1:4-5**
        2. Predicted (prophesied)
        3. Came without warning. (People were not specifically praying for it.)
        4. Languages
        5. Purpose: to usher in the Kingdom with power

    **B.** Accounts of the baptism with the Holy Spirit

        1. To the Jews-in Jerusalem (**Acts 2**)

        2. To the Gentiles-begins with Cornelius (**Acts 10**)

            a. Note: Cornelius and his household were water baptized in v. 48, saved at baptism.
            b. Peter explained actions to the Jews (**Acts 11:1-18**).
            c. "At the beginning," (**Acts 11:15**)

    **C.** Does the Baptism with the Holy Spirit still exist today? **Ephesians 4:4-6**: There is one baptism-which one? (Written about 60-62 A.D.) There are three options:

1. John's baptism-passed when new covenant began (**Acts 19:1-5**).

2. The baptism with the Holy Spirit (**Acts 2 and 10**). No longer present as it was a prophecy/promise that has been fulfilled. It was never a general command for all Christians.

3. Baptism with water in the name of Jesus Christ for the forgiveness of sins to receive the indwelling of the Holy Spirit.

   a. Jesus commanded this baptism (**Matthew 28:18-20**).
   b. This baptism is recorded all the way through the book of Acts and the epistles. **1 Peter 3:21** (also written around 62 a.d.) makes reference to this water baptism of salvation.
   c. It had to be the one baptism of **Ephesians 4:4-6** as it was the only one practiced by 60-62 A.D. when Ephesians was written.

## 3. The miraculous gifts of the Holy Spirit (next lesson).

Received by the apostles' laying on of hands

No longer present today

# MIRACULOUS GIFTS OF THE HOLY SPIRIT

**1. TYPES OF MIRACULOUS GIFTS**
  **A. 1 Corinthians 12:8-10**

      1. Wisdom
      2. Knowledge
      3. Faith
      4. Healing
      5. Miracles
      6. Prophecy
      7. Distinguishing Spirits
      8. Tongues
      9. Interpretation
  **B. (Mark 16:16-18)** Some will be able to:

      1. Drink poison and not die
      2. Be bitten by snakes and not die **(Acts 28:5)**

**2. TYPES OF "LAYING ON OF HANDS":**
  **A.** Blessing **(Acts 13:3)**
  **B.** Healing
      1. Ananias heals Paul's blindness **(Acts 9:17-18)**.
      2. Paul heals Publius' father on Malta **(Acts 28:8)**.
  **C.** Passing on the Gifts
      1. Apostles would pass on the gifts **(Acts 8:18)**.
      2. These people could not pass on the gifts they received.
         a. **Acts 6:1-8**: Context is the choosing of "The Seven". This is the first occasion that the gifts were passed. Stephen immediately starts to perform miraculous signs among the people with God's power (v. 8).
         b. **Acts 8:1-25**: Context is after Stephen's martyrdom. Great persecution breaks out. Many leave, but apostles stay in Jerusalem.

Philip, one of the seven who had received the gifts in **Acts 6:1-8**, goes to Samaria. He performs many miraculous signs and healings to get people to believe (v. 12), including Simon the Sorcerer (v. 13) and they are baptized. (They became Christians and thus receive the forgiveness of sins and the gift (indwelling) of the Holy Spirit, **Acts 2:38**.) When apostles come to Samaria, Simon saw the Spirit's gifts were only given by apostles' laying on of hands and offers them money for the ability (**Acts 8:18**). Note: Simon didn't ask Philip for the gifts because Philip could not pass them on. Simon is rebuked for having the wrong motivation.

   c.  **Acts 19:1-6**: Paul finds disciples in Ephesus who didn't know what the Holy Spirit was because they had only received John's baptism of repentance. Then they were baptized into the name of Jesus Christ to receive the forgiveness of their sins and the indwelling of the Holy Spirit (v.5). Then they receive the miraculous gifts of prophecy and speaking in tongues by the laying on of Paul's hands (v.6). Paul is an apostle.

## 3. GENERAL OBSERVATIONS

   **A.** Apostles were able to pass on the gifts because they were apostles. The Apostles possessed the ability to perform miracles even during the ministry of Christ (**Luke 9:1**). This ability to pass and perform the gifts were not given at Pentecost.

   **B.** **1 Corinthians 12 and 14** are not the directives on how to receive tongues (the church there had already received them), but rather the correctives on how to use them because everyone was speaking at the same time and misusing the tongues. **1 Corinthians 12:28-30** shows that tongues as a gift were not given to everyone in the church. Thus the concept of a "Pentecostal church" (every member speaking in tongues) is against scripture.

C. **1 Corinthians 13:8-10**. "Perfection" here could not mean the coming of Christ because it is in the neuter gender in Greek, not the masculine gender. When perfection comes probably refers to the canonization of the Bible sometime after the first century. At that time, all the miraculous gifts would be gone because all the apostles and those to whom they passed the gifts would have died.

D. The purpose of the miraculous gifts from **1 Corinthians 14:20-22**
  1. To get non-believers to believe (tongues were only to be used to bring non-believers to faith.)
  2. To edify the Christians and strengthen their faith.
  3. Now the Bible fulfills these needs-thus the church today does not need apostles or miraculous gifts.

E. **2 Thessalonians 2:9-10** shows there can be miracles by Satan today. Satan's purpose is to deceive people about the truth, so they will not be saved.

F. Speaking in "tongues" is common in many religions (Mormon, Catholic, Islam, etc.) because religion gets dried and staid. These are also called "ecstatic utterances"-non-understandable sounds and fragments of speech.

G. A person can be filled with the Spirit without speaking in tongues (**Ephesians 5:18-19**).

H. Jesus never spoke in tongues and he was accorded the full-measure of the Spirit (**John 3:34-36**).

# THE CHURCH

1. **Colossians 1:15-18**
   The church is the body of Christ. The body needs the head. The church is essential to Christianity.

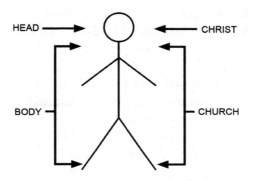

2. **Ephesians 2:19-21**
   **A.** The church is the family of God.

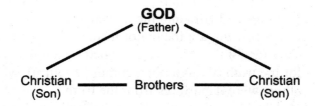

   **B.** **1 Corinthians 12:12-13**: baptized into the body of Christ, the church
   **C.** **Romans 6:3 - 4** teaches we are also baptized into Christ. Baptism is when we become a christian, a son of God, and at that same point we become members of the church, the family of God.

3. **Ephesians 2:20**
   **Cornerstone: Christ**
   **Foundation: Apostles and Prophets**
   > Apostles = New Testament Bible

Prophets = Old Testament

The church is based on the Word of God only.

4. Have you ever wondered why there are so many denominations? (450 or more exist in the U.S. alone.)
   A. The Bible teaches there is one church.
      1. **Ephesians 4:4-6** – One Body
      2. **Romans 12:4-5** – One Body
      3. **1 Corinthians 12:12-13** – One Body
   B. Divisions in Christendom are either of Satan or of God.
      1. **1 Corinthians 1:10-13** Division is sin, when following personalities and in time their writings (traditions of men that contradict the Word – false doctrines). **Matthew 15:6-9**
      2. **Luke 12:51-53**; **John 10:19-21** Division will occur and is righteous, when an individual, church or movement aligns themselves with the Word of God. The Jews considered themselves "God's people," yet Jesus' words (the truth) divided them into two groups – those who opposed Him and those who obeyed Him.
   C. The following are the major historical divisions in Christendom – some were formed by a noble stand for the truth (though not a complete return), while others were departures from the truth.
      1. Through the centuries the church was corrupted by traditions of men – false doctrines, such as: infant baptism, original sin, perpetual virginity of Mary, priests as clergy, papal infallibility, etc... This becomes the **Catholic Church**. In 364 AD the Roman Empire is split into two parts. This division leads to a split in Christianity – the eastern portion becomes **Eastern Orthodox Church** and the western part becomes the **Roman Catholic Church**. Practices diverge, for example – Orthodox has married priests, Roman Catholic priests are celibate. The "Great Schism" occurs in 1054

266

AD, as the leaders of "each church" excommunicate each other.

2. **1500's Reformation Movement** – Martin Luther (Lutheran Church) He takes a stand against the Roman Catholic Church on these convictions: Bible authority over church authority, salvation by faith not works, and the priesthood of all believers, yet still baptizes infants. Other noted reformers were John Calvin (Presbyterian Church), Ulrich Zwingli and Conrad Grebel (Anabaptists) Anabaptists were heavily persecuted by Catholics and some reformers, because of their stand for adult baptism. Henry VIII (Anglican Church / Church of England) He breaks from the Catholic Church over his right to divorce his wife. He appoints himself head of the church. Later in the United States, the Anglican Church becomes the Episcopalian Church, since members will not follow the king of England.

3. **1700's Great Awakening Movement** – John and Charles Wesley (Methodist Church) Followers divide from Church of England over: personal transforming decision for Christ not state religion, high accountability of members, and preaching to the "unchurched;" also practiced infant baptism.

4. **1800's Restoration Movement** – Alexander Campbell and Barton Stone (Mainline Church of Christ and Conservative Christian Church) Take a stand against both Catholic and Protestant doctrines of salvation. They preach to be saved one must have personal faith in Christ, repentance and baptism (immersion) for the forgiveness of sin to receive the Holy

Spirit. In reaction to Catholicism, their congregations are autonomous – self-governing. (1906 is the formal split between Mainline Church of Christ, which is non-instrumental, and the Conservative Christian Church, which is instrumental.) Joseph Smith (Mormon Church) divides from Restoration Movement in 1830 over "new revelation" – the Book of Mormon.

5. **1967 Crossroads Movement** (Total Commitment Movement) Controversial, though never departing from the Mainline Church of Christ, the Crossroads Church near the University of Florida pioneers evangelizing the secular campuses of United States, "counting the cost" with each person that desires to be baptized, and the shepherding of new converts.

6. **1979 Boston Movement** (International Church of Christ) – Kip McKean – Baptized at the University of Florida in 1972, divides from Mainline Churches of Christ and Crossroads Movement over: Bible Church not just New Testament Church, only disciples are true Christians, each and every member of church must be a disciple, each member should be in discipling relationships, vision to evangelize the nations in a generation, the planting of new churches to achieve this vision, central leadership not autonomous congregations, and the role of women. In 2002, the International Churches of Christ return to a more Mainline Church of Christ theology – each congregation becomes autonomous (self-governing), calling a central leadership and the vision to evangelize the nations in a generation

268

"unbiblical." Around the world, thousands fall-away.

7. **2006 SoldOut Movement** (Portland Movement / International Christian Church) Begins in Portland, Oregon as a revival movement within the International Churches of Christ. The International Church of Christ separates from the SoldOut Movement, because of the new movement's stand on these convictions: Bible Church not just New Testament Church, only disciples are true Christians, each and every member of church must be a disciple, each member should be in discipling relationships, vision to evangelize the nations in a generation, the planting of new churches to achieve this vision, central leadership not autonomous congregations, and the role of women.

5. What is the "one church?"
   A. **Acts 11:25-26 Church = Disciples = Christians** When God looks down from heaven, He sees one church – all the baptized disciples around the world, who are "sold-out" in obeying His Word. This is called the "church universal" – the one true church. (Ephesians 4:4-6)
   B. A local congregation is called the "visible church." In the first century, all the "visible churches" made up the "church universal." However, since so many "visible churches" have departed from true doctrine and because all sold-out baptized disciples are not in one fellowship, we should strive to be a member of a local congregation.
   C. The Greek word for church is "ekklesia" which means "assembly" or "called out". ("Ek" meaning "out" and "kaleo" meaning "to call.") To be a disciple is to be "called out" from the world.

Therefore, the church in the Bible was the "assembly" of the "called out."

   **D.** There are several names in the Bible for God's Church: Disciples, Christians, Church of God, Church of Christ, The Way, Church of the Firstborn, Saints, etc… Since we are free to choose any name for our fellowship, since our fellowship goes around the world, and because our churches

6. **What distinguishes the International Christian Churches? (What separates or "divides" us from mainstream Christendom?)**
      **A. We believe God physically resurrected Jesus from the dead.**
      **B. We believe the Bible is inspired by God and is our sole authority.** Therefore, since we have not departed (divided) from the truth, we consider ourselves non-denominational.
      **C. We are a Bible Church, not simply a New Testament Church. 2 Timothy 3:14-17**
   The context of the word "Scripture" is referring to the Old Testament. We believe the Old Testament applies to our lives – as much as the New Testament – except for the Mosaic Law and any teaching in the New Testament that supersedes the Old Testament. (Example: grounds for divorce)
      **D. We believe – as in the book of Acts – the visible church should be composed of only sold-out baptized disciples.**
      **E. "Be silent where the Bible speaks, and speak where the Bible is silent."** In applying Scriptural principles to build the visible church, we believe we must obey God's Word, but where the Bible does not prohibit a practice or name, we are free to use our God-given creativity. **Genesis 2:19** (Examples: The principles for "Bible Talks," "Lead Evangelist," "Discipleship Partners" and "Regions" are in the Scriptures, though these terms are not.

However, nowhere are they prohibited. Also, instrumental music and paid Women's Ministry Leaders are not prohibited in the Scriptures.)

F. **We believe in a Central Leadership.** Throughout God's Word, when His people were unified, there was a strong central leadership and godly central leader. (Examples: Moses, Joshua, David and of course Jesus and the Apostles) **1 Corinthians 4:15-17** and **Titus 1:5** teaches that local congregations had an overseeing evangelist, who unified the disciples "everywhere in every church." In the first century, congregations were a collective movement – not autonomous, not self-governing.)

G. **Matthew 28:19-20 Our vision – the evangelization of all nations in this generation –** will be accomplished through every disciple making disciples and every disciple having discipling relationships.

7. **1 Corinthians 12:14-27**
   A. We need the body. The body needs us (v. 21).
   B. Be involved on a relationship level in the church (v. 26).

8. **Hebrews 10:23-25**
   A. Do not miss church.
   B. The fellowship helps us to be unswerving in our commitment (v. 23).
   C. Another purpose of fellowship is to encourage each other so we will remain faithful (**v. 24**)
   D. Must come to all meeting of the body: i.e. Sunday and midweek services, special devotionals, Bible jubilees, retreats, seminars, etc. Begin to rearrange schedule to come to all the meetings of the body.

9. **Contribution**
   A. **Malachi 3:6-12** Do not rob God in your tithes and offerings. Tithing is the guideline for our sacrifice

271

on Sundays to meet the ministry needs. Benevolent offerings are given at Midweek Services.

**B.** **2 Corinthians 9:6-8** Giving should be from a "cheerful" heart – not under compulsion

**C.** God blesses you when you sacrifice

# FOLLOW-UP STUDY #1
# AFTER BAPTISM, NOW WHAT?

**INTRODUCTION**

  **A.** Discuss: first few days as a Christian.

  **B.** Share "letter to God." If the new disciple has not had a chance to write one, encourage him/her to do so.

**1.  Acts 2:36-47 – The Conversion of the 3000**

  **A.** Discuss Biblical Conversion

   **1.** Review how to become a Christian.

   **2.** Reinforce the joy of salvation.

  **B.** Devoted to the Apostles' Teaching – the Word

   **1.** For a quiet time, suggest a book or theme – reading a chapter a day.

   **2.** For many, a quiet time journal is helpful.

  **C.** Devoted to Fellowship

   **1.** Discuss the purpose of each gathering: Sunday Worship Services, Midweek Services, Devotionals and discipleship partners.

   **2.** Discuss the need to initiate relationships – give not just receive.

   **3.** Discuss the importance of hospitality – invite people into your home for a meal.

   **4.** Discuss the expectation to tithe on Sundays and give a benevolent offering at the midweek services. Read together **Malachi 3:6-12** and **Hebrews 13:17**.

  **D.** Devoted to Breaking Bread – Communion **(1 Corinthians 11:23-32)**

   **1.** Discuss purpose of bread and fruit of the vine.

   **2.** Discuss what it means to become spiritually "Weak, sick and fallen asleep" How does communion prevent these conditions? (sick: **Proverbs 3:12**)

  **E.** Devoted to Prayer

273

       1. Discuss how prayer brings peace.
       **(Philippians 4:4-7)**
       2. Share petitions and answered prayers.

2. The Conversion of Paul **(Acts 9:18-25)**
   A. Paul immediately begins to preach.
       1. Who have you shared with?
       2. List people to share with.
   B. Paul grows powerful.
   C. Paul is persecuted.

3. **Hebrews 5:11 – 6:6 The First Principles**
   A. Strive to learn the first principles (elementary teachings) and go on to maturity, so you can be fruitful and not fall away.
   B. Discuss taking The First Principle Classes

# FOLLOW-UP STUDY #2
# CHRIST IS YOUR LIFE

**Introduction**

    **A.** Discuss:
- 1. Did you have daily quiet times this past week?
- 2. Who did you share with and invite?
- 3. Did you feel good about your level of sacrifice in time and money?

    **B.** Discuss the impact of communion on Sunday.

**1. Colossians 3:1-4 – Raised to a New Life**

    **A.** Raised with Christ in baptism (**Colossians 2:12**)

    **B.** Set your mind (thoughts) and set your heart (emotions) on things above.

    **C.** Christ is your life.

**2. Colossians 3:5-11 – Put to Death**

    **A.** Be open about your greatest struggles this week.

    **B.** Discuss practical ways to crucify these sins.

**3. Colossians 3:12-14 – Put On – Clothe Yourself**

    **A.** Compassion

    **B.** Kindness

    **C.** Humility

    **D.** Gentleness

    **E.** Patience

**4. Colossians 3:15-4:1 – New Attitudes**

    **A.** Peace (v. 15)

    **B.** Thankful (vv. 15-16)

    **C.** Wholehearted (v. 17)

    **D.** Family interaction (v. 18-21)

    **E.** Employer-employee relationship (3:22, 4:1)

    **F.** Teacher-student relationship

# FOLLOW-UP STUDY #3
# BEST FRIENDS OF ALL TIME

**Introduction**

    **A.** Share about your closest relationships during your life – God and spiritual family in comparison to your physical family and old friends

    **B.** Ask the young Christian, "Who are your Closest Friends?"

**1. One Another Scriptures**

    **A. John 13:34-35** Love one another. Jesus teaches that Christians should have better relationships than people in the world. Set your mind to make the Christians around you your best friends.

    **B. Hebrews 3:12-14** Daily encouragement of one another

    **C. Ephesians 5:19-20** Worship God with one another – sing out to God each other with psalms, hymns, and spiritual songs

    **D. Colossians 1:28-29** Disciple one another. The is essential in God's plan to become mature. As we mature, we learn to instruct one another (**Romans 15:14)**

    **E. Galatians 6:1-2** Gently restore one another and bear one another's burdens

    **F. James 5:16** Confess sins to one another. Discuss openness and transparency, remembering that "openness breeds openness," so share your struggles

    **G. James 5:16-18** Pray for one another – it makes a difference!

    **H. Hebrews 12:14-15** Be holy and prevent "bad attitudes" in one another

    **I. 1 Thessalonians 5:12-14** Outlook towards one another.

**J. John 17:20, 23** The ultimate goal of love and unity
   – world evangelism


2. **Date and Marry Only Disciples**
   A. **1 Corinthians 7:39** Marriage must be in the Lord.
   B. **2 Corinthians 6:14-18** Dating, as is marriage is a
      partnership, where you are "yoked together."
      Disciples must separate from unbelievers to
      receive the promises of God.
   C. **1 Kings 11:1-10; Nehemiah 13:23-27** Study this
      principle in the Old Testament. To date or marry
      outside of the faith is to be unfaithful to God. If
      you are single, have you gone on a Christian Date?
   D. **1 Peter 3:1-7** If you are married, are you winning
      your spouse?

3. **Reconcile with One Another**
   A. **Matthew 18:15-17** Christians will sin against
      each other. When someone sins against you, do not
      gossip by going to someone else. Talk to the
      person who hurt you, so you can win him/her over
      as a friend
   B. Church discipline begins one-on-one and rarely
      should go to steps 2, 3 and 4

# FOLLOW-UP STUDY #4
# THE MISSION

**Introduction**
    **A.** Share about the visitors you most recently brought to church or Bible Talk.
    **B.** Ask the young disciple about their evangelism.

**1. Jesus' Mission**
    **A.** Luke 19:10
    **B.** 1 Timothy 1:15
    **C.** Matthew 28:19-20
    **D.** Acts 20:24
        **1.** What was Jesus' mission?
        **2.** What is each disciple's mission?

**2. Disciples Mission**
    **A.** John 15:1-16
        **1.** Glorifying God in **John 15** is bearing the fruit of making disciples, not simply baptizing. (**Matthew 28:19** commands us to "go and make disciples;" **John 15:16** commands us to "go and bear fruit that will last.")
        **2.** To bear fruit, one must be "in the vine," otherwise we will be cut off.
        **3.** Jesus is the perfect discipler, but He is also the perfect disciple of God.
        **4.** To love God is to obey His commands. Discipling helps our hearts to want to obey His commands. (**Matthew 28:20**) Therefore, we must love one another, even to the point of laying down our lives for each other.
    **B.** The Book of Acts records the 30 years from the beginning of the church on the day of Pentecost to Paul's arrival in Rome – signaling that the gospel has gone to the known world. The church in the

first century was a movement. Discuss the growth of the first century church when all Christians were striving to be fruitful – making disciples.

| | |
|---|---|
| **1. Acts 2:41** | **9. Acts 11:21** |
| **2. Acts 2:47** | **10. Acts 12:24** |
| **3. Acts 4:4** | **11. Acts 13:49** |
| **4. Acts 5:14** | **12. Acts 14:1** |
| **5. Acts 6:1** | **13. Acts 14:21** |
| **6. Acts 6:7** | **14. Acts 16:5** |
| **7. Acts 8:4** | **15. Acts 17:4** |
| **8. Acts 9:31** | |

**16. Acts 17:6 (RSV)** "These men who have turned the world upside-down have come here also…"

**17. Colossians 1:6, 23** The known world was evangelized by 61 AD, in a generation! (Paul is in prison when he writes **Colossians – Acts 28.**) Therefore, Jesus' vision became a reality – "the evangelization of the nations in a generation!"

**C. Discuss and pray for:**
1. World Evangelism
2. Mission Teams
3. Your Kingdom dreams… how can you use your talents for God?

# FOLLOW-UP STUDY #5
# PERSECUTION*

**Introduction – 2 Timothy 3:12 Everyone who wants to live as a disciple will be persecuted.**

1. **Jesus was persecuted.**
   A. **Family**
      1. **Mark 3:20-21** Jesus' family thought he was out of His mind. (brain-washed; mind-control)
      2. **Mark 3:31-35** Jesus prioritized His spiritual family above His physical family.
      3. **Acts 1:12-14** This conviction produces conflict. However, after His resurrection and ascension, His mother and brothers were disciples.
   B. **Gossip and slander**
      1. **John 7:12-13** Jesus was accused of deceiving people.
      2. **John 10:19-21** The Jews – religious people – intensely persecuted Jesus through name-calling and character assassination. Jesus' teaching always divided His listeners.
   C. **Scope of persecution**
      1. **Luke 23:1-3** Jesus is condemned to a death by crucifixion through half-truths.
      2. Jesus – who was perfect – was falsely accused and misunderstood by His family and killed by religious leaders. What do you think will happen to you if you follow Jesus?

2. **The First Century Church was persecuted.**
   A. **Acts 5:17-18, 38-42**
      1. The Jewish leadership arrested the apostles for preaching the Word, because of jealousy.

*\* This study has been proven to be most helpful after the Discipleship Study. KM*

280

    2. Those who persecuted the Christians thought they were doing this for God, though in fact they were fighting against Him.

    3. The apostles suffered physical mistreatment.

    4. Persecution did not stop the disciples from daily proclamation.

**B. Acts 28:21-22**

    1. Everywhere, the church was highly controversial.

    2. The church was called a "sect." (cult)

    3. Since the International Christian Churches have the goal of imitating Jesus and the first century church, what will happen to us? If a church is not being persecuted, what does that imply?

3. **Causes of persecution. 1 Timothy 4:16 – Life and Doctrine**

**A. Life**

    1. **1 Peter 4:3-4** The world feels condemned by those who no longer participate in its sin.

    2. **1 Peter 4:12-16** Do not be surprised or ashamed by persecution, but be sure you are persecuted for righteousness sake.

**B. Doctrine**

    1. Preaching the Word – **John 15:18-20; 16:1-4**

      a. Jesus warns that persecution comes to those who preach the same message as Him.

      b. Jesus warns that the price of hatred is certain, and perhaps even death.

    2. Narrow Road of Salvation – **Matthew 7:13-14**

      a. Acts 4:12 Only an individual who believes in Jesus is saved.
(This truth condemns atheists, polytheists, Jews, Muslims, Hindus, Buddhists, etc...)

      b. Acts 2:36-38 Only an adult who is water baptized for the forgiveness of sins is saved.

(This truth condemns those who practice infant baptism and "praying Jesus into your heart" as doctrines of salvation.)

c. **Matthew 28:19-20** Only the person who makes the decision to be baptized as a disciple is saved. (This truth condemns those who may baptize for remission of sins, but are not made into disciples before and after baptism.)

d. We do not condemn the lost, they are condemned already. However, when the lost are confronted doctrinally about their condition before God, they will repent, run or persecute.

C. **Doctrine of discipling - Matthew 28:19-20**

1. **Matthew 28:19-20** Discipling, calling people to obey the Word of God, is often viewed by the world as controlling.

4. **Our attitude about persecution**

A. **Matthew 5:10-12**

1. Do not fear persecution. Do not care what men think about you, only God.

2. Rejoice! You are not alone, since they persecuted both Jesus and the prophets.

B. **Ephesians 6:10-18**

1. Satan is behind all persecution. Only God and His spiritual armor will give you the victory over the world.

2. **Conclusion** – The International Christian Churches are a controversial Christian movement. Some call us a cult and accuse us of both brain-washing and mind-control. Many false rumors and half-truths have been spread. Newspaper articles, television shows and especially the internet have slandered the ICC, and yet, the facts are that lives have been radically changed, marriages have been healed, drug addicts have been freed, the poor

have been fed and cared for, and this rapidly growing movement – The SoldOut Movement – is spreading around the world in this generation! Just like the first century!

**(See caicc.net, usd21.org and The Chronicles of Modern-Day Christianity)**